CISTERCIAN STUDIES SERIES: NUMBER ONE

No Moment Too Small

CISTERCIAN STUDIES SERIES: NUMBER ONE HUNDRED FIFTY-THREE

No Moment Too Small

Rhythms of Silence, Prayer, and Holy Reading

Norvene Vest

CISTERCIAN PUBLICATIONS
Kalamazoo, Michigan

COWLEY PUBLICATIONS
Boston, Massachusetts

Library of Congress Cataloging-in-Publication Data:
Vest, Norvene.
    No moment too small: rhythms of silence, prayer, and holy reading/
Norvene Vest.
       p.   cm. —(Cistercian studies series; no. 153)
    Includes bibliographical references.
    ISBN: 0 87907 653 4 (Cistercian: alk. paper)
    ISBN: 1-56101-092-8 (Cowley: alk. paper)
    1. Benedict, Saint, Abbot of Monte Cassino. Regula. 2. Benedictines—Spiritual life. 3. Spiritual life—Catholic Church. 4. Catholic Church—Doctrines. I. Title. II. Series.
BX3004.A2 1994b
255'.106—dc20   94-436 CIP

Scripture quotations are taken from the *New Revised Standard Version* of the Bible, © 1989 by the Division of Christian Education of the National Council of the Churches of Christ in the United States.

The detail on the cover is taken from *The Kitchenmaid* by Jan Vermeer, and is used by permission of the Rijksmuseum in Amsterdam.

This book is printed on recycled, acid-free paper and was produced in the United States of America.

Cistercian Publications
WMU Station
Kalamazoo, Michigan 49008
The work of Cistercian Publications is made possible in part by support from Western Michigan University to the Institute of Cistercian Studies.

Cowley Publications
28 Temple Place
Boston, Massachusetts 02111

Contents

Acknowledgments

I am full of gratitude to Benedict, Scholastica, and their many spiritual sons and daughters through the centuries who have tended the hearth fire of this way of the gospel, and who have helped me along the way. In particular, my grateful thanks go to all the monks of St. Andrew's Abbey, Valyermo, California, where I am an oblate. My life is immeasurably enriched by Abbot Francis Benedict and Fr. Luke Dysinger, who meet monthly with my husband and me to pray and to share visions and tasks.

I am especially indebted to Fr. Luke Dysinger for his collegial partnership in developing a contemporary model of the Benedictine spirit suitable for both monastics and non-monks. I am also grateful for his translation of the Rule of St. Benedict, which I use here as I did in my commentary on the Rule, *Preferring Christ,* and to Source Books who published that commentary and translation in 1991. Both have graciously given permission to quote from it.

I also owe considerable thanks to Rozanne Elder at Cistercian Publications, who persisted through many revisions in thinking this book worth publishing, and to Cynthia Shattuck at Cowley Publications for welcoming the opportunity to co-publish.

Foundations

Some ten years ago I began going on occasional retreats to a Benedictine monastery. From the outset I sensed that the monks had something special, something I'd like to have. But I thought that in order to "have" Benedictine spirituality, I would need to renounce the world, give up married and professional life and my home, and "abandon all" for Christ. Unwilling to do all that, I nonetheless continued my periodic retreats, and each time returned to my own setting refreshed and renewed.

Gradually I began not only to talk to the monks about their life in the monastery, but also to read about Benedict himself. Benedict lived in the late fifth and early sixth centuries, from approximately 480 to 547. Born in an area called Nursia in Italy, he died as abbot of Monte Cassino, a large monastery he founded south of Rome. Our only knowledge about his life is provided by Book Two of Pope Gregory the Great's four-book *Dialogues*. Benedict's Rule, his most enduring legacy, was written during the approximately twenty-five-year period he was abbot of Monte Cassino, that is, around 525 to 550.[1]

The Rule at first puzzled me by its brevity and its homeliness. But, like the monastery where I made my retreats, it continued to attract me, and I kept returning to it, each time a little more ready to hear it speak. Gradually the Rule began to shape my own prayer and to pose questions about my own life. The Rule coaxed and invited me, not to abandon all, but rather to embrace all, even while offering it daily back to God. It began to teach me ways of orienting my life to Christ, of putting Christ at the center of everything. I found many of my earlier ideas about Benedictine spirituality turned upside down. Benedictines are not basically solitary; they are persons living in community. They are not renouncing the world as something evil, but are loving God's creation by not grasping it. They are not so much set apart from other people, as set near the presence of God. They are not superhuman persons, but are fully human persons willing each day to *be* human in God's sight. They are often wrong and confused and full of pride, and they welcome God into their lives exactly as they are.

Slowly it dawned on me how relevant this way of thinking and living was to my own life. Gradually I have come to realize how healing and humanizing the Benedictine way could be for every Christian living in the world. That is the vision I seek to share in *No Moment Too Small.*

Benedict's call is different from what we might expect of an ancient ascetic. It is not so much a giving up, a renunciation, as an attentiveness to what we are given in each day's experience. The specific problems we find hard in daily life can become a means of receiving God. In effect, Benedict begins his rule with a loving invitation much like this: "Listen, my children, with the ear of your heart, and you will have life!" Do we know what life really is? Can we imagine abundant life breaking into the next hour of our day? What would it look like? How would it feel? How would we recognize it? What difference would it make to us? All these are the questions of wisdom: how can I live? Perhaps we expect that the spiritual life will be dramatic, or peaceful, or overwhelmingly pure; perhaps such dreams prevent us from turning with gladness to the dreary, familiar routines of our own settings in a way that lets us see what has been there, waiting for our attention, all along.

Something New and Something Old

Monastics living under the Benedictine Rule have long been aware of its balanced emphasis on both solitude and community, on both moments of prayer and acts of charity. Yet this practical approach to God through the ordinary has not been much highlighted in written discussions of Benedictine spirituality in the past. Possibly it did not seem necessary, because until recently someone attracted by the spirituality of the Rule and wanting to know more about its way of living would be told: "Join us! Come live with us in the cloister and see." Benedict's application of gospel principles to practical daily life were then made naturally in the context of life together. This response is, of course, the hospitable answer of Jesus in John 1:39 and Matthew 4:19: "Come. Let us love God together."

In our time, the Spirit seems to be stimulating another response. Many persons who live outside the monastic setting and feel called to remain there are experiencing a deep longing to join men and women monastics in their particular way of loving God. Religious have been generous in encouraging such extended communities of "Benedictines in the world," but new questions are raised in these encounters. How can we articulate the essentials of Benedictine spirituality in a way that does not depend on cloistered life? How can the foundational elements of this path of the ordinary be described in ways relevant to people who live in Los Angeles or Washington, raising families or committed to jobs ranging from real estate development to computer software to child care to psychotherapy?

The attractiveness of the Benedictine way to people in the world is that it *does* have simple, direct, and profound advice for ordinary lives. Yet in order to appropriate this advice, we worldlings must first engage in a process of exploring Benedictine spirituality with those who have been formed by it in the cloister. We may then draw out from their insights some of the essentials which transcend and yet address our particular circumstances today. As we translate the Rule to include those not in the cloister, what do we discover is essential? How can the centuries-old wisdom of Benedictine spirituality be relevant to those living in the twentieth-century world? Which of its characteristics best empower us to practical living of the gospel in the circumstances of our lives? How does the Rule help me, whoever and wherever I am, to be a better Christian, to live more in fidelity to my baptismal vocation?

The Ordinary

The key to Benedictine spirituality lies in the word "ordinary." Benedict insists that no moment is too small for nearness to God. Life in Christ does not necessarily involve something dramatic or heroic. It may simply engage the everyday stuff of my life, which Benedict suggests is what actually matters. Christian living is daily. Everything in my life matters. Whatever my present circumstances, Christ will meet me there. However confused, bewildering, boring, or chaotic my life, God is involved in it right now. No matter how little or how much I think I love and serve God, God is waiting, ready to deepen our relationship. The fullness of life in Christ is meant for me, wherever and however I am. Benedict's Rule teaches me how I can respond to God's presence more readily here and now.

It has been said that the only portions of the Rule that are helpful today are its very first chapters on prayer: the first seven chapters of the Rule set the "spiritual foundations" and the next twelve lay out the daily office of prayer. The remaining fifty-four chapters discuss liturgical details and administrative organization in the monastery, matters that are sometimes considered too specific to their own time to be of much help to us now. Yet this point of view reinforces the separation between life and prayer, which is exactly the split Benedict intended to heal. The later chapters of the Rule are in some ways the most fruitful for us today, for they show how Benedict applied his spiritual theology to matters of ordinary life. The specifics of his life and ours do vary, but the principles he used to deal with small matters can be enormously helpful to us, if we can but coax them out of his text.

In response to an irate demand, can we speak lovingly? When we have made a mistake, do we defend ourselves and blame others, or are we willing to admit our error and apologize at once? When we begin a new task, do we depend entirely on our own strength or do we ask God's help? Are we sufficiently sensitive to the needs of others that we will pass the bread in response to a mere nod? How do we care for old clothes or garden tools? When we experience weakness in others, are we disappointed that they have let us down, or do we gladly offer them our strength, knowing that we can depend on theirs in other circumstances? These are the ordinary, practical matters that Benedict draws together into a life dedicated to God. It matters very much what each of us does with daily choices.

In the Rule, Benedict teaches us to see the dynamic center of our lives as the application of our desire to serve God within the give-and-take of our days: in manual labor and cleaning up, in making and selling our creative products, in taking care of the old and the young, and above all in living together. The joy of

Benedict's spirituality lies in learning to see our routines as filled with God's presence.

This book will explore silence, holy reading, and prayer. I begin with these topics because Benedict understood them to be the foundations of daily Christian life. Silence, Scripture reading, and prayer. We know those words well. But have we found them to be radiant sources of life? Perhaps we do not understand the words as well as we think, or understand them as Benedict did. Often, in dealing with the Rule, we should assume at first that we have no idea what familiar words mean, for the context in which they were used is often foreign to our present experience.

As we explore the particular way of meditating on Scripture that Benedictines call *lectio divina* (holy or godly reading), for example, we discover that "reading" means something very different from our quick scanning of printed matter. We may think we can readily understand the term by substituting the modern phrase "Bible study" or even "exegesis," yet these are far from what Benedict meant. If we rest in our assumptions without looking carefully at a term's use in the Rule, we are likely to find ourselves bewildered by Benedict's instructions. The power of the Rule will increase when we can begin to encounter old words as if they were new, letting Benedict's different understanding gradually sink in and form our responses. We may discover something that helps us deepen our awareness of what is going on in our lives. We may find new vitality in familiar practices and discover that old, comfortable expressions of faith become stimulating encounters with God.

Benedictine spirituality is rooted in a movement from hearing to response to transformation. This movement resembles a helix, with one element spiraling endlessly into another. When hearing is attentive, it leads naturally to self-giving response. When the response is generous, it includes a surrender to God that allows God to effect inner change. The three foundational elements of Benedictine spirituality—silence, holy reading, and prayer—are included in this unified movement. Yet, because we usually approach hearing and response as two separate acts and regard transformation as nearly impossible, each element is handled in a separate chapter in this book. Benedictine silence is paired with hearing, or attentive listening. Benedictine reflection on Scripture is viewed primarily as response to God. And Benedictine prayer is presented as a means of transformation.

Benedictine spirituality is founded in silence, holy reading, and prayer not only because these elements describe the movement by which ordinary life can become abundantly God-filled, but also because as he handles them, Benedict illumines other dimensions of life, including relationships and work. An appreciation of Benedict's insights into the way in which silence, holy reading, and prayer are inextricably mingled in daily life may provide special benefit for people who experience their lives as fragmented into unrelated categories of work, family, religion, recreation, or study.

We may know theological truths in our minds, but the essence of Benedictine spirituality requires that we learn to perceive and respond to these truths each day. Benedictine spirituality is intended to be lived, to be a practical guide that enables us to be who God created us to be: unique men and women who belong to Christ. The foundational elements of the Rule enable us to give heightened attention to the presence of the holy within our ordinary daily experience, no matter how superficial the event. All three elements are centered in expectant listening to what is, response to God then and there, and openness to God's work in us through ordinary events.

Benedict's foundations teach us to live fully, in regular and joyful communication with the ineffable and the mysterious Godhead. God is alive in us as we experience silence, as we read in a godly manner, and as we pray. Our spirit is being formed, slowly and steadily, by that Spirit who lives in our deepest being. We must shift our analogy from one of foundation to one of formation, for silence, holy reading, and prayer will shape us. Think of a potter, molding clay by the gentle pressure of hand and wheel. If we let God mold us, we become what God created us from all eternity to be.

When through exercises we develop these attentive skills, God is enlarging our hearts, making them generous and capable of receiving all that has been intended for us. Let us become receptive to this divine activity within our hearts. God initiates the divine-human encounter, and although our first activity must be receptivity, we are required to make an effort, to involve our feelings, intellect, and will. By them we gradually move toward (or away from) the love of Christ in every moment of the day.

Each chapter in this book presents one of Benedict's foundational elements by discussing the principle contained in the Rule and then posing questions about issues related directly to the modern reader's experience. The relationship of these two aspects varies in each chapter, but each is always present. The movement is always from principles to practical application for modern life in the world, reflecting Benedict's desire to unite prayer and life into an integrated whole. In this interactive way, I hope to show that the themes in the Rule can become relevant to and useful for today's Christians as they seek help for the concrete difficulties they face in their life journeys. Each chapter ends with exercises that may be used by individuals or groups to help apply Benedict's Rule to their own situations.

No Moment Too Small explores Benedictine spirituality as a useful, practical guide for persons in the modern world. The Benedictine way offers a balanced way of life for people who long for intimacy with God and yet find themselves distracted and immersed in practical duties and problems. It is my belief that the recovery of this ancient spirituality for all Christians may help satisfy the hunger many of us feel for an authentic Christian life, lived *in* the world but not *of* it.

Endnotes

1. Gregory's Book Two has been published in English under the title *The Life and Miracles of St. Benedict,* translated by Odo J. Zimmermann, osb, and Benedict R. Avery, osb (Collegeville, Minn.: The Liturgical Press, 1949). The most widely available modern translation of Benedict's Rule in English is that presented in *RB 1980: The Rule of St. Benedict in Latin and English with Notes,* Timothy Fry, osb, General Editor (Collegeville, Minn.: The Liturgical Press, 1981).

Chapter One

Silence

J f our surroundings and our minds are stuffed with noise, how can we hear? If our cup is already full, how can it receive anything else? If we think that every possession must be earned or claimed, how can we be receptive to even the most generous gift offered us? To hear, to receive, to accept: silence invites us to these. To learn the listening art of Benedict's Rule, we need silence. Accepting silence is the first step toward intimacy with God.

We cannot listen if we are surrounded by noise. Hearing requires silence. There is so much noise in our modern world that we may not at first realize how much we need silence in order to hear. Yet all of us have experienced the frustration of trying to tell someone something important with the television set blaring or a loud conversation going on across the room. When we think about it, we realize that genuine listening, listening with a desire to hear, requires silence. True conversation, even and especially between those who love each other, requires silence. God, the great Lover, invites us into silence in order to draw forth our response to his Word.

Strangely enough, we moderns, who experience so little silence, often think that silence is easy. We who are so noise-addicted believe that silence is something anyone can claim readily—until we try it. Being silent is an art to be learned, much like playing baseball or speaking a language. We need regular practice to become comfortable and proficient in the art of being silent, and in our culture we are woefully out of practice. Instead of seeking to befriend silence, we generally run away from it. We are so accustomed to the prevalence of noise that we feel uneasy without it; our lives are shaped by the hum of freeway traffic, the undertone of music on telephones and in restaurants, the continual repetition of headline news, and even the private din of personal headphones. We regard noise as normal, and silence as an aberration. By and large, we deliberately keep silence at arm's length, even though we may not be conscious of this. As we compulsively or carelessly switch on our television sets, we are avoiding silence. At some level we sense its radical power to show us how incomplete we are without a loving relationship with God.

Does this sketch seem unfair? Would it seem to be easy for someone raised in our culture to slip into silence at will? Try this experiment. Put away this book for a while. Turn off the radio and television and any other artificial noise in your immediate environment. Ask any family members or co-workers not to disturb you. Close the doors and windows of a comfortable room, and enjoy fifteen minutes of silence. Just listen to and in the silence, and welcome it. Most of us will find this experiment very difficult. We have no idea how alienated we have become from the simple presence of silence.

Yet the Rule of Saint Benedict does not urge that we become silent just for the sake of being silent. Benedict does not give an absolute value to silence; he gives it importance in relation to the Word of God. Think of the story of Elijah in the Hebrew Scriptures (1 Kings 19:9-13), which Benedict would have heard read aloud regularly at the night office. Elijah had wearily come up on the mountain to meet God. At first, he was principally aware of flashy, dramatic events: earthquake, strong wind, and fire. Only gradually did he become aware that God was not in these things. And finally, Elijah was receptive to the still, small voice that brought him reassurance. Though God can express the divine presence in mighty acts, we often hear the voice we need in stillness.

Silence and the Word

Between word and noise there is a distinction. When we capitalize Word, we know that it refers to the Word of God: Jesus Christ and Scripture. Christ the Word and Scripture, God's Word, are not hostile to silence. Indeed, they seem almost to have been formed in silence and given forth as natural and harmonious extensions of silence. There are words we can speak that exist in rhythmic congruence with silence. These words have little in common with the noise of our culture, which so impudently endeavors to overwhelm and suppress silence. In his Rule Benedict sought to minimize noise and to maximize Word (including the human words formed in the silence of God's presence).

It is clear in the Rule that silence is intended to foster listening. Silence is not valued for itself, as some sort of magic tool. Rather, silence creates an environment in which God can be heard and welcomed. At the root of Benedict's guidance on silence lies the conviction that God is continuously revealed through the medium of our experience. Silence helps us to be aware of this constant presence, and to allow it to shape our speech and action.

The Rule begins with the word "listen," and immediately promises that if we attend with the ear of our hearts, faithfully practicing this listening, we will be brought back into that immediate relationship with God from which we have drifted. Benedict continues to rouse us to this task: "It is time now...to hear with wondering ears what the Divine Voice admonishes us, daily crying out." The Rule urges us to listen and respond to God's call each and every day: "The Scripture stirs us up.... Run while you have the light of life....What can be sweeter?" (RB Prologue:8-19).

Some may take this call to mean that they must flee their present environment and escape into a hermitage where they can devote themselves to silence, but this is not its primary meaning. Rather, the Rule asks Christians to practice regular silence in order that we may learn to hear the voice of God within our ordinary situations. Once we have been formed in hearing the Word, we are gradually able to express it naturally in our own lives. The Word becomes a vital and transforming part of our experience. But it takes patience and a gentle receptivity to be so formed in silent attentiveness. Thus we encounter the paradox that we need to withdraw with regularity from busy-ness and noise for a time, precisely so that we can more fully appreciate the possibilities for words of truth and life within our usual settings.

Silence fosters dialogue and ongoing communion with God within each day. It invites us to ask whether anything in our own daily rounds can be holy. Is God active in *my* life? Must I set my ordinary routine aside to be near God? Must I leave God behind when I am occupied with the usual activities of my life?

The fundamental Christian affirmation particularly highlighted in Benedictine spirituality is the Incarnation. The taking flesh of God in Christ is an invitation to see God everywhere. Incarnation as a theological principle means not just that God once took actual, temporal, material form, but that God can be found everywhere, all the time, within everything. God is not contained within but revealed through the material. Outward form is not unimportant, for the material form has been created by God for a specific purpose. We are invited to look with awe at each person and thing, for in some mysterious way, Christ shines forth from each. The world in which we live is a medium for the divine revelation. There is a continuous and creative interpenetration of the spiritual and the material in all of created reality.

Benedict's understanding of God is extraordinarily broad and generous. Not only does silence teach us to hear God in such "spiritual" resources as Scripture and religious tradition, but it also invites us to hear God in such apparently mundane things as visitors and boring works. Benedict teaches that all guests are to be received as Christ, and blessing may be asked of them (RB 53:1, 24). Brothers gently encourage each other as they drowsily arise for night prayers (RB 22:8). There is no prohibition against speaking during working hours, pre-sumably because "during work, the Word of God comes to a monk through the interaction of brothers."[1]

Benedict perceives God as present immediately and actively within the ordinary materials and interactions of each day. Every encounter, every incident during the day is grist for the mill of the ongoing God-human commu-nication. No activity is too small or too unimportant to mediate the holy. Living one's faith this way results in a much deepened attentiveness to each moment, for we learn that the specific ordinariness of a thing or a person also reveals a more "dense" reality, that is, its glory. Benedict's Rule always celebrates the simple daily inter-actions of one person with another, and of human hand with pot and pan, all as potentially carrying a wonderful message.

Most of the time, we don't see the glory of ordinary things. In general, the presence of the divine in our lives is not only mysterious, but downright opaque. The con-necting spiritual membrane is murky, blurred, obscure. How can we become more aware of God in our day-to-day routine? How can we sense God present in our lives more often? What might help us see things as we believe they really are in the times and the places of our lives? Silence. The discipline of silence gives us a foundation on which to orient our lives to the reality of the Divine Presence that we know by faith is with us always.

Benedict's silence enabled him to understand how God speaks within the daily round in a way that is vital, dynamic, and immediate. For Benedict, the Word of God was a person, a presence, someone living and active who permeated his whole daily experience. That Word, subtle yet powerful, waits everywhere for our welcome. In the Rule, silence provides a way of hearing and greeting this quickening Word. Silence gives us a way of allowing the Word to abide in our hearts until it changes us. Let's look at how silence is encouraged in the Rule.

The Rule requires total silence during the night and economy of words in the daytime. Obviously, those of us outside the cloister will not normally be able to experience so full a round of silence, because our practical duties at work and at home oblige us to speak. Despite this constraint, we need not abandon the Rule's helpful guidance on silence. If we ponder the details of Benedict's silence in the Rule, we discover underlying principles that can help us modify our lifestyle so as to allow silence to become a more creative influence in ordinary moments. But we need to attend reflectively, for Benedict was very succinct in his instructions on silence.[2] He encourages us to moderate our speech and to be particularly aware that those who accept their own discipleship do well to listen more than speak. When we are eager to learn anything, we listen. When we want very much to know the ways of God, we also listen. "There are times," counsels Benedict, "when we ought to refrain even from good words for the sake of silence" (RB 6:2).

The idea that we are not to speak because silence has value in itself may surprise us. We might readily agree that it is better to be silent than to speak a harsh or angry or malicious word. But not to speak even a good word? What value does silence have that might so commend it? Reflecting on this, we come gradually to see that speaking is a way of asserting control and avoiding receptivity.

By practicing silence, we allow ourselves to be taught by God's presence. Listening, we are opened to the gifts God may be offering us and others in this moment. We expand our capacity to receive what is beyond our power to provide. Hospice workers and those who visit the sick and the dying quickly learn the art of holding back even good words in order to invite more fully the creative presence of the healing Word into their midst. To know how not to speak at crucial moments, they practice the wisdom of silence at ordinary ones. These care-givers know that silence orients them toward hearing.

Benedict would have us be hearers of God in ordinary as well as extraordinary moments. The complete silence his Rule requires at mealtimes is illuminating in this respect. Silence at meals was routine in monastic communities of Benedict's time, but his emphasis differs from that of most of his contemporaries.[3] Benedict calls for silence not for the negative purpose of stopping conversation (which might give rise either to arguments or bawdiness), but for the positive purpose of listening to the Word of God, particularly in the Bible or in the Church Fathers. Yet reading is not the only means to God's Word. Benedict urges his monks also to be attentive to each others' needs as they eat and drink, and to the superior's words of instruction (RB 38:5-9). For Benedict, the completely ordinary events of the day are filled with God. God is equally present in the silence, in the reading, in the fellowship of the meal, in the way monastics are attentive to each other's needs. But it is silence that allows attentiveness to the transforming Presence in all details of each moment.

Learning Silence

We have said that the discipline of silence for monks of ancient times that the Rule outlines also has relevance for contemporary life in the world. How might we apply silence outside the monastery? Begin with an awareness that silence is not an easy discipline for those living in our culture. Be careful not to overcommit yourself initially, yet begin to notice opportunities within your everyday settings to practice silence. What about an occasional coffee break alone, perhaps just slipping down to the foyer or a garden in the entry patio and sitting quietly for five minutes? Could we take different streets driving home from the office, allowing a few more minutes for the ride on a less crowded route, enjoying the solitude of sixty seconds at a stoplight? Some work tasks offer a silence of simple absorption. While folding the laundry or sanding a board we can consciously appreciate being attuned with natural rhythms of breath or heartbeat.

It is helpful for us to arrange periodically for longer and more deliberate times of silence to let silence seep into our being, reorienting ourselves in the listening stance of a disciple. We might explore silence occasionally through an entire afternoon working in the garden or wandering alone in a city park. We might register for a weekend at a local monastery or retreat house. Following the experience of several extended periods of silence, we might adopt a regular practice of spending a few hours or a day during a week or month in the discipline of verbal silence. In following such practices, it is well to be sensitive both to the silence and to the improved capacity for listening we develop as silence expands our receptivity to God.

Exploring the Rule and its spirituality even further, we discover ever more challenging forms of silence that can benefit modern secular lives. Various forms of silence implicit in the Rule include: silence of environment and body; silence of tongue; and active interior silence. We will now explore each of these practices of silence in turn.

Silence of the environment and body

In our early experiments with silence, we focus on exterior silence. We eliminate or minimize all noise in our environment, not only speech but even music or machinery, during certain regular periods of time. The limitation of exterior noise creates an outer framework of silence. In an urban setting, this outer silence is difficult to achieve. Yet we can begin simply. Switch off the radio, television, and non-essential electrical appliances. Close the windows. If possible, get out into the country or deep into a park, away from mechanical and verbal noise. Detach from technology. Simply stop. Even these basic actions may constitute a major effort for some in our noise-pervaded culture.

Silence of the environment also includes the immediate physical environment, which is our body. We may take it for granted that the body is silent, but in fact it can be very intrusive. Even our bodies express noise addiction. If we arrive early at a public meeting and sit quietly and listen, for example, we become aware of how much commotion people make as they take their seats.

Contrast this experience with that of meditating in a monastic chapel before the daily office: the monks slip into their seats so quietly that we may not even be aware anyone else is present. Similarly, our attentiveness in a business meeting may reveal to us that many people are unable to sit in repose for even so short a time as fifteen minutes without fidgeting or shifting. Most of us cannot walk through a forest without making a great deal of noise. We have lost the art of bodily silence, of harmonic and peaceful physical presence with the created world of which we are a part. The practice of bodily silence may be as valuable an asset to prayer as turning off the television.

Those aware of the attention given to the body and its silent receptivity in eastern religions often do not associate this attitude with Christianity. Yet the Benedictine way of life did indeed provide for attention to the body. The monastic cloister has for many centuries been known as the "gateway to God" because it was the passageway between the monks' sleeping quarters and the chapel, but it also served as an exercise ground for the development of a natural bodily silence based on the rhythms of breath and heart. As the monastics trod this rectangular path day after day, their bodies became attuned to a rhythmic serenity that assisted attentiveness to God.

Physical meditative walking, in contrast to sitting, is part of the basic Benedictine discipline of bodily silence. During the day, monks and nuns would usually take a few moments to pace several times around the cloister, softly repeating a phrase from the morning's readings, thus memorizing the words of Scripture and letting them become a thing known by heart. Routinely engaging the body in the rhythmic, meditative exercise of *lectio divina* helps the body find its natural silence, while also relaxing it and opening up mind and spirit. The practice of meditative walking is faithful to Benedict's insistence on avoiding "heroic" asceticism and focusing instead on what anyone can do in a few moments during the day or week. Walking lets us enjoy the body's natural rhythms while creating a deepened silence in our immediate environment through peacefulness in our own body.

Silence of the tongue

Silence of the tongue is a special kind of exterior silence, and holds a privileged place in the Judeo-Christian tradition. The early monastics appropriated a long biblical heritage in seeking to control speech as a spiritual discipline. Benedict considered the tongue to be an abusive instrument that any person serious about the spiritual life must restrain. Like Scripture, his Rule emphasized that "death and life are in the power of the tongue," insisting that much talk makes it difficult to avoid sin (RB 6:4-5). Compare Benedict's words with those from the Letter of James, for example: "If any think they are religious, and do not bridle their tongues but deceive their hearts, their religion is worthless" (James 1:26).

It is not hard for us to see that we do more harm than good by passing along gossip, by barbed and pointed repartee, by angry outbursts. Silence of the tongue requires that we seriously repent of and eliminate such behavior from our lives. There are two reasons for this. One is charity: it is hurtful to abuse or slander one's neighbor. The second, however, is holiness: a sharp tongue is a sign of wickedness, a spiritual poison, within the slanderer. Jesus warns that the things which come out of us—words revealing a bitter, arrogant, or lustful heart—endanger our souls (Mark 7:15). We are urged to discipline our tongues not only to avoid hurting others, but also to avoid personal sin.

Even knowing this, we find it hard to recapture a keen sense of the value of verbal silence when our culture encourages us to say exactly what we think. Yet both approaches express a commitment to truthfulness: modern psychologists and monastic writers alike observe that a busy tongue is often the way we *hide* from the truth about ourselves.

Silence of the tongue reveals much about our motive for speech, if we pay attention. Before we speak, we can pause to choose silence and then look honestly at what the urge to speak is telling us about ourselves. Often we discover that we are trying to manipulate someone, to control results. Do we focus on someone else's error in order to direct attention away from our own? Expressing anger may be easier than bearing grief or hurt, and more honest communication may reveal our need. Are we using words to cover up something? Are we dependent on words to express ourselves? We may use words to divert others from perceiving our real feelings, because we fear that if people know what we are really like, they might not be sympathetic. Is talk a lame effort to make things right, rather than simply to admit and share the fact of great pain? All these little dishonesties close off the passageway to God and block receptivity to Christ. Words can be ways of hiding from the Word, rather than means of allowing ourselves to be formed by it. How often we use language to avoid truth rather than accept it and let it teach us what we need to know!

Silence of tongue involves more than the avoidance of talk, which can aid us in observing ourselves and our motivations. Silence is a way "to open a passageway...to the ebb and flow of the eternal Word" in our midst.[4] Silence frees us to hear and respond to Christ here and now. When we acknowledge the pettiness and defensiveness of much of our speech, we can admit how much we need the help of the Holy Spirit to allow words to be born from a healing silence deep within us. The absence of words can free us to attune ourselves better to Someone beyond words.

A period of silence may change the quality of the words we do speak. When we are able to be honest about why and how we use words, then we have choices. On further reflection, we may find that our fear of disapproval is an unwanted fetter. We may choose to reveal a bit more of ourselves on the risk that a more authentic self may be valued more rather than less. By waiting a moment before we speak, we may choose to affirm what is cherished in another rather than to pick at minor habits. With silent reflection, we may decide the time is right to say a word about how important our Christian faith is to us.

Silence helps us turn away from sin and toward God, choosing to speak in love toward ourselves, our neighbors, and God. Within the discipline of silence we can become established in God, so that our few words can express the compassion that is the mark of God's presence.

Active interior silence

In practicing exterior silence, we notice two apparently contradictory results. On the one hand, we observe that our bodies can lead our minds and spirits into greater receptivity for interior silence. And on the other hand, the cessation of exterior sound may simply heighten awareness of considerable inner noise. We discover that our minds are seldom silent, and they seem to grow noisier in proportion to increased exterior silence.

In many spiritual disciplines, we are advised to ignore these inner voices, releasing them at once to move fully into complete silence. The Benedictine tradition has a more subtle and nuanced approach, in which we are neither expected to leap into deep inner silence nor urged to set aside all distractions at once. Rather, we are encouraged to receive the interior noises as an invitation to hard work: we are to be attentive to distractions as opportunities for movement toward or away from God. Benedict warned his readers:

> Keep guard at all times over the actions of your life, knowing for certain that God sees you everywhere. Dash down at the feet of Christ your evil thoughts, the instant that they come into your heart; and lay them open to your spiritual father. (RB 4:48-50)

Benedict also recommended that his disciples read the *Conferences* and *Institutes* of John Cassian. There they would find instruction on dealing with wrongful thoughts and inner distractions (RB 73:5). These books, compiled by Cassian on the basis of his fourth-century conversations with Christian *abbas* in the Egyptian desert, were regularly read in Benedictine monasteries at mealtime.

Mental distraction was one of Cassian's primary concerns in his conversations with the Egyptian *abbas*. Cassian complained:

> I have only got far enough to know what I cannot be....Insensibly the mind returns to its previous wandering thoughts and slips back with a more violent rush, and is taken up with daily distractions and incessantly

drawn away by numberless things that take it captive, so that...all these observances seem useless.[5]

Young Cassian despaired of his inability to attain inner silence, but he was advised to welcome inner disturbance as the occasion for analysis of thoughts, motivation, and choices for or against God. He drew his systematic approach to handling inner disturbances from the *Praktikos* ("The Practical Life") of Evagrius Ponticus. Evagrius analyzed eight basic patterns of inner noise common to those seeking God, framing the problem simply:

> There are eight general and basic categories of thoughts in which are included every thought. First is that of gluttony, then impurity, avarice, sadness, anger, *acedia*, vainglory, and last of all, pride. It is not in our power to determine whether we are disturbed by these thoughts, but it is up to us to decide if they are to linger within us or not and whether or not they are to stir up our passions.[6]

Benedict transmitted Cassian's approach to practical inner work as a primary ingredient in monastic formation.

The Benedictine tradition suggests that interior noise can usually be understood to express basic human predispositions of gluttony, lust (impurity), greed (avarice), and other vices or failings. Such thoughts occur to everyone, but disciples can choose how to handle inner voices so as to support rather than disrupt their journey with God. When we are attentive to inner noise, we frequently observe that we are preoccupied with food, sex, and possessions. Benedictine spirituality urges the importance of becoming aware of inner themes that typically dominate our thoughts in silence, so that we can work with them.

Silence can help us discover what our inner voices have insidiously been suggesting to us all along. In silence, we can work with interior distraction, exploring the source and direction of these often hidden inner voices. We alternate between carefully listening to our inner noise and releasing it into the restful silence of God. We gain perspective on the interior nagging talk that often fragments us. Active silence involves an inner rhythm of attention and release, encounter and rest, acting and offering. The Benedictine way creates a balance of silence and word: it does not aim at absolute silence, nor does it reject inner noise in silence as a sign of failure, but sees it instead as a sign of life, when it is accepted as God's invitation to us to work toward interior freedom.

We may initially hesitate to consider silence as an active interior discipline, particularly if we have thought of silence as passive rather than active, and total rather than rhythmic. Yet this Benedictine view can provide real comfort when we find ourselves confronted with the strong inner turmoil that so often accompanies exterior silence. The increase of inner noise can be frightening if we do not expect it. We may feel that we are doing something other than spiritual work, and that ordinary concerns are unsuitable for attention in our time with God. If so, the Benedictine tradition encourages us to take heart and be glad for all the secrets and struggles now presenting themselves to us before God. Silence creates an environment in which we can attend carefully to ourselves as a part of God's created world, seeing God's transforming presence in our own inner noise no less than elsewhere.

Many of us find silence difficult because we interpret it as cruel, hostile, or angry. In our past, important persons may have used silence as punishment for "bad" behavior. People often refuse to speak as a way of hurting someone, so silence may seem to carry the negative connotations of being scolded. How often we hear someone say, "We're not speaking to each other" but mean, "We're very angry with each other." Silence can bring memories of a withdrawal by someone with whom we had been seeking deeper intimacy; thus silence may embody a painful refusal of our self-offering. If our primary experience of silence in the past has been isolating, exterior silence may open us anew to a painful sense of unworthiness.

In silence, we may also find ourselves face-to-face with memories of times we have turned away from God or acted harshly to someone. Silence may confront us with the ways our own brokenness has caused us to hurt others or exalt our own ego. We may suddenly remember running roughshod over someone's feelings, or taking what we felt we needed although we knew it rightfully belonged to another. We may realize we have substituted sex for intimacy, and used and defrauded our partner. We may recall spewing venom all over a family member rather than facing the hard work of reconciliation. Silence invites us to accept responsibility for our own lives and actions.

And silence can remind us of unresolved past experiences, exposing a sense of vulnerability. If there is a painful incident in our past with which we have not fully come to terms, such as the death of a loved one, it may well surface in silence, seeking attention and the necessary mourning of loss. Perhaps some earlier life circumstance was too hard for us to deal with at the time, and we have never forgiven ourselves or others. These burdens cannot be avoided in silence; they will surface for attention and healing.

Courage and the insights of a sensitive tradition are necessary for us to persevere with the practice of silence. Without them, we may run away when we encounter this silence/non-silence, because we feel vulnerable, grief-stricken, full of pain, or exposed. We may feel isolated and fearful and be tempted to flee at once back to busy-ness and noise to avoid the difficult emotions that demand our attention. The point is that all these elements arise when we stop running and talking because they are real and they are present. The deepest levels of our self-awareness are very much preoccupied with questions of fundamental worthiness, integrity, and vulnerability. In various ways we have all sought to express and find affirmation for these precious aspects of ourselves in the world; in this broken world, all of us have been wounded.

For healing of these wounds, we need God's love as well as the love of others, but we are often afraid to risk it. Is God there? Is God good? Dare we trust our faith, when our wholeness rests on a transformation beyond our powers? The Benedictine view of silence encourages us to explore this rhythmic interplay between allowing honest doubts and fears and needs to surface in us, and offering them to God, who we believe can heal them. When the "noise" of anger, desire, or hope is presented to God, some exchange occurs which makes a difference to us. We are angry, and we breathe. We desire, and we offer. We are anxious, and we rest. We are always placing our life before God for transformation and then receiving what God gives back.

Can silence really cause beneficial change in our lives? We cannot know until we open ourselves to God and accept the possibility. There is no way to receive comfort until we have acknowledged our need. Yet we have the assurance of centuries of Benedictines who have tested this method and found peace of mind. Until we stop in silence to be aware of who and how we really are, we have not offered our true selves to God. And we have not risked discovering our emerging selves in God. In time, the discipline of active interior silence will bring us deep into the heart of God where we are whole.

Practicing Active Interior Silence

If we wish to apply the Benedictine discipline of active interior silence, how may we go about it? What practical steps can be gleaned from the tradition? A pattern can be drawn from the Benedictine sources for our own work: first, be attentive; second, explore alternatives; third, seek help; fourth, remain patient; and fifth, accept new life. We will explore each of these steps in turn, noting as we begin that the sequence is somewhat artificial. In reality, the steps all merge into a continuum of experience in which different elements predominate at different times, yet always in the rhythmic interplay of silence and word, of activity and receptivity. Taken together, these five elements describe Benedictine active interior silence in terms that help us apply the practice in our own lives.

1. Be attentive

First, we seek to notice and become objective observers of the interior noise that arises in silence. We seek to be aware of what is really there when we stop long enough to listen. Gradually, as we are attentive and relaxed, these noises will sort themselves into patterns of repeated messages. Until we become still and start to listen, we may never be aware of the content of our own inner messages, often telling us such hurtful or foolish things as "There you go, failing once again!" or "How selfish and inconsiderate you are" or "Just one little lie can't hurt anything" or "Everybody else skims off a little extra; why shouldn't you?" or "Your life is so painful, boring, wearying; why keep carrying on?" When we look at these messages, they often seem quite at variance with what we consciously think; and yet their guerilla tactics give them a disproportionate interior emotional power. We begin silence's active interior discipline with the simple but courageous willingness to become aware of what is really going on in us.

2. Explore alternatives

The second step is to gain insight into alternatives to the negative or sinful inner messages. Christian tradition teaches that every vice has a corresponding virtue. While that language may or may not be helpful to us, it is useful to consider alternative inner messages we could substitute. For example, if our usual inner voice accuses us of failure, we might deliberately address that voice with a statement from Scripture or tradition that counteracts it, such as "Jesus came to heal the sick, not the well" (Matt. 9:12). With that conviction, a different alternative than failure can be affirmed. Each time we hear ourselves saying: "I'm a failure," we can immediately substitute the message: "I made a mistake, but I am still loved, and there is help for me." And whether or not we *feel* that the alternative is true, we can believe it on faith and endeavor to incline ourselves in that direction.

Perhaps the use of these affirmations sounds overly simple or childlike, but it rests in a wise understanding of the human spirit. The tradition acknowledges that a repetitive inner nagging voice that erodes our sense of self-worth is a *pathe,* a disorder, which separates us from God. It forms a debilitating pattern which can keep us from God when we feel unworthy of God's care. After we become aware of our thoughts, we are to seek alternative thoughts to substitute for them. In seeking alternatives, we affirm that God has indeed created us in the divine image and likeness and calls us to wholeness, even as we feel far from it.

Lust and anger were two of the major disorders of concern to the monastic tradition. A look at alternatives to these passionate emotions may help us, for the tradition sought not to suppress troubling thoughts, but rather to offer them for consecration to God. Evagrius saw the vice of lust as a positive indication of the human ability to be attracted to something beyond oneself.[7] An openness to being powerfully called beyond oneself is essential for response to one who loves us, as God does.

Evagrius reminds us that we are creatures of God, made as God intended. Therefore our desires must have some positive purpose. When we stay with our reality in the silence, seeking understanding, we may observe that our longing for another tells us something not only about the way we were made but also about the nature of our Maker. When we observe lust in ourselves, we can accept it as a sign of our desire for intimacy and union, however painful it may be to know that we are incomplete, in need of union. We endure the truth. We can then "incline our hearts" in a new way (Ps. 119:112; cf. RB Prologue:1). In the case of lust, we can redirect our longing toward God, where it can be met by the only One capable of satisfying us. Only with God's love at the center of our being can lust be converted to love: abiding in God, we know ourselves to be lovable and able genuinely to love others.

Or perhaps we observe anger in ourselves. Again, Benedictine active interior silence acknowledges the truth that we all experience anger. Living with that truth, we sense that although anger is destructive when bitterly turned against another, it can nonetheless point to something inherently good in our human nature. We need not push away anger, but can mentally choose to redirect it against the inner voices that would tell us we are worthless. Anger fires us with the positive strength to overcome evil with good. We can incline ourselves to direct our anger not against others or against our own essence, but rather against those inner impulses which try to defeat our attempts to honor the life God has given us. We enlist our anger to place us before God rather than to separate us from God.

Seeking alternatives is the first step of repentance, in its basic meaning of "turning away from." We turn away from our inner compulsions met in silence first by becoming aware of them, and second by becoming aware of alternatives. We repent when we believe we are called to something better and more whole, when we see that the new possibility invites our best efforts. Repentance involves exploring mental patterns met in silence until we gradually learn how best to redirect them. Alternatives enable us to see that basically good, natural, and human impulses go wrong when they are self-directed rather than God-filled. The alternative, or new inclination, aims at creating an ongoing disposition toward God.

3. Seek help

The third step in practicing the Benedictine discipline of active interior silence involves asking for help. It may seem to us that the practice of silence has a great many words! Can we really call this a discipline of silence when so much activity is involved in it? We noted earlier that Benedictine silence involves a rhythm of word and silence, and this means that the discipline involves not only our intellectual efforts but also an element of receptivity. What has been described so far sounds very much like modern behavioral or cognitive therapy, which is often helpful but has its limitations. We cannot think or feel or will ourselves into wholeness. We can cleanse the wound and set the bone, but healing comes as a gift and in its own time. In the repentance of exploring alternatives, we do what we can. And on the heels of that repentance, we are confronted with the limits of our capacity and the need to seek help beyond ourselves.

This step of seeking help is suggested by Benedict when he talks about tears in prayer: "Go in with simplicity and pray, not with a loud voice, but with tears and fervor of heart" (RB 52:4). Our tears express intense inner desire for something we are unable alone to effect. In tears, we are earnestly asking God to provide what is beyond our capacity.

Benedict's direct insight into active interior silence comes largely in chapter 4 of his Rule, "The Tools of Good Works." It begins with the command that undergirds everything that follows:

> In the first place to love the Lord God with all your heart, all your soul, and all your strength. Then to love your neighbor as yourself. (RB 4:1-2; Mark 12:30-31)

This is a succinct summary of the goal of active interior silence: love—of God, of others, of self—is the motivating force of Christian life. All our work with inner faults, sins, and compulsions is intended to lead us to greater love. Benedict and those who followed in his tradition were committed to exploring those outer and inner habits that increase our ability to live in fidelity to this command of our Lord.

The discipline of interior silence is not an accounting system by which we proceed step by step, converting one vice after another into a virtue. Silence aims at letting us leap into fullness of life, at accepting our God-given ability to be *like* God in that we are able to will the good for every living thing. This challenge is captured in a story from the desert *abbas*. A monk comes to Abba Joseph and says that he is faithful to his little rule—what more should he do? The *abba* raises his ten fingers, aflame with the power of the Holy Spirit, and replies "If you will, you can become all flame."[8]

Benedict's tradition invites us, through the discipline of silence, to become living flames, to allow ourselves to be so penetrated by the life of God that we reveal in our own being the presence of God's kingdom. We are called to be loving, to be whole, to be so filled with God that God's glory pours through us. Yet we cannot make ourselves into this living flame. Silence as discipline brings us to the monk/seeker's discovery: transformation does not happen because we do more, but because we allow God to work in us. Nothing in our power enables us to make the dramatic shift from elimination of a few faults to the life of abundance to which we are called and for which we long. This awareness of personal incapacity is one of the essential gifts of silence.

Today we are quite well aware that our faults are often caused by our wounds. Abused children tend to become abusive parents; greedy adults were often starving children. Those who once were completely powerless have become arrogant dictators. Often we sin against others precisely in the ways we have been sinned against. Accordingly, it may be difficult to repent genuinely of our faults, especially if our behavior has developed as a defense against too great a vulnerability. We will not release negative behaviors, however much we may think we choose to do so, if we believe that they are essential to our safety.

Lust, anger, and pride are all defenses designed to shore up a vulnerable sense of self. We have often heard it said that the best defense is a good offense. How much simpler to respond in anger to the bearer of bad tidings than to confess our part in the creation of a difficult situation! How easy it is to indulge in anonymous sexual encounters because we are frightened of the almost mystical power of genuine sexual intimacy. If we fear that God is dead, how much simpler to create massive human artificial environments than to face our own desperate longing and loneliness. Any fault or vice is more than just a defense against vulnerability; equally clearly, there are dimensions of self-defense in any vice.

When we seek to repent of our vices without considering the role of vulnerability and incapacity, we inevitably reach an early dead-end. We simply seize upon some form of personal discipline which will collapse periodically rather than ask God's help to free us from dependence on a protective vice. In time, the pattern of discipline and collapse becomes intractable, if we do not acknowledge our helplessness to break it by our efforts alone. Until we face the reality of our own genuine need for nurture from some source outside ourselves, until we allow ourselves to know we are hungry and thirsty, we can never have the freedom to *choose* fasting in a starving world. Unless we accept the truth of our own vulnerability and limitation, we will not have the inner strength to choose God's peace in a violence-prone world. And strangely, it is often easier to acknowledge that we have sinned than it is to admit that we need help to avoid future sin.

Yet we reach a point in the spiritual journey when the primary task is to acknowledge and accept our inability to proceed further on our own resources. We must acknowledge the impossibility of becoming the living flames we long to be. We must come to see the painfulness of our desire to live in fullness of life with God, because we humans are inevitably incomplete, wounded, not whole. We cannot create for ourselves the reality for which we most long. This realization occurs at the third step in active interior silence, and here our words slip away into tears. To ask for help does not require words so much as a sense of need and loss. We cannot repent as we would like. We cannot transform ourselves. We cannot, by our own strength, love God, self, or neighbor as we would. And yet we cannot give up longing for the fullness promised in relationship with God.

Our prayer becomes a sob, our silence becomes a wordless cry. Benedict assures us that "we shall be heard, not for our much speaking, but for our purity of heart and tears of compunction" (RB 20:3). Cassian's friend, Germanus, cries out at one point: "I am desirous of stirring myself up with all my power to conviction and tears." Gregory of Nyssa urges tears as "the deluge [falling on] sins, the purification of the world." Tears express a mourning for lost salvation, for separation from God, for the lack of perfection from which our best efforts somehow always fall short. Tears express the confession that no one can love or do good, without help beyond nature.[9]

Dissolving into tears is not the same as being immobilized by one's own incapacity to live without sin. When we ponder our faults and vulnerabilities and stay only within the framework of our own responsibility and guilt, we find ourselves so overwhelmed by our human weakness that we do feel paralyzed. The gift of tears takes us beyond this paralysis. Tears cry to God for help, which God always gives even before we call (RB Prologue:18). As a twelfth-century son of Benedict, Bernard of Clairvaux, wrote,

> As long as I look at myself I see nothing but what grieves me. But once I look up and raise my eyes towards God and [God's] pitying help, the glad sight of God soon makes up for the sad sight of myself....Such is the experience and sequence of getting to know God as one's helper: first, one finds oneself in need of help, and second, one calls to the Lord and he listens....In this way self-knowledge leads to the knowledge of God.[10]

Tears somehow carry us beyond the limitations of ourselves, beyond faults and even beyond virtues. Tears carry us through our own helplessness beyond ourselves to God, where alone we find the strength that can enable us to become what we desire. Benedict urges us to welcome tears as a *blessing*, a sign of mourning for the wholeness which we so desire yet are unable to create for ourselves. It is neither easy nor comfortable to stay with this moment, and yet we are encouraged to do so. The discipline of silence invites us to respond to this honest (if appalling) vision of who we are by continuing to hold it before our eyes even as they fill with tears. We are not to flee into distractions, but to let the silence heighten in us the truth of what we see. Our willingness to stay in this discomfort, to remain aware, to weep for what we see—are all means by which we ask for help and welcome God's power into our silence.

4. Remain patient

Having asked for help, we wait. At this fourth step we persist in what we can do and trust in God for what we cannot do. Healing, wholeness, transformation all take time. Patience is required for what may seem a time of darkness and obscurity. Generally, we are not aware of movement toward light and health; we feel nothing is happening. We have acknowledged our deep longing, and for a time we live in the bleak discomfort this awareness of desire and emptiness and inability brings.

The map provided by the Benedictine tradition may comfort us at this point. It suggests that God is at work in us, whether or not we are aware of it. We are to put our hope in God, and never to despair of God's mercy (RB 4:41,74). We know that it is the Lord, not ourselves, that brings about good through us, and that we are encouraged to pray that God will bring our work to perfection (RB Prologue 4:29). So this step in the discipline of silence offers a time for us to be quiet, to rest in confidence that God is doing all that is necessary. We are to be willing finally to rest. We cease comment and turn in wordless trust to God.

Both Evagrius and Cassian speak of our activity as preparation for contemplation, while the more pragmatic Benedict seems to suggest an ongoing rhythmic interplay of action and contemplation in ordinary daily life. All three agree that at some point in the spiritual practice of silence we stop even our mentally active encounter and wait on God. When we have done all we can to allow our individual enslaving thoughts to surface, to recognize and admit them and offer them for transformation, we then let go, entrusting everything to God. We may imagine ourselves holding an offering plate high and having it received into the clouds. We offer these secrets of our deepest self, and God receives them from us. We are relieved of everything, and we can release it, at least temporarily, into God's accepting hands.

If the monastic tradition of engagement with silence is not identical with other religious traditions that insist on strict silence, neither is it exactly like the modern psychotherapeutic model of healing. Benedictine silence insists on an essential element of wordless surrender. Unique to the process of monastic waiting is the offering up of all we have discovered. We are encouraged to seek understanding, but at the last we turn to God, giving over all that troubles us or gives us pleasure into God's will.

In Benedictine silence, we seek God. We ask God to form us into the person God calls us to be. We seek self-knowledge and abundant life in Christ through active pursuit, and all our activity is initiated and permeated by God's grace. In response to God's call and as best we can, we admit and repent and remedy. And then we acknowledge our special need for God's help to be carried across the yawning chasm into new life. Having been busy with activity, we now slip receptively into deep silence and wait. We believe that our effort to choose God in all things will be honored; we can become what we desire and affirm because of God's promise and grace. We cooperate with what is possible by giving the very stuff of our lives to God in this moment, as completely as we can. We return it all. We offer. We wait in silence.

Sometimes when we cease our personal struggles and turn our faults and vulnerabilities over to God, we sense no response at all. We experience God as absent. With Jesus on the cross, we cry out: "My God, why have you forsaken me?" We sense profound abandonment and aloneness, an isolation that terrifies.

At this moment of apparent isolation, our loneliness can be eased by the faith of the community which is greater than our own. In our sense of the absence of God, we cannot rely solely on personal experience. Like so much in this journey into silence, the wisdom of others, here beside us and gone before us, is of great value. We learn the discipline of active interior silence best in the context of a community of others who are likewise on the journey toward and with God. We are helped by others who recognize from their own experience similar inner patterns and fears. We build up our own strength as we gain confidence that others share our purposes and our struggles. We learn to recognize small signs others commend in us, and to rest in God's peace. Even with a continuing sense of isolation, we know we are not alone, and we have company on the narrow way (RB Prologue:48).

In the Rule, silence is never separated from the whole life of the community, living together in faithful journey. Benedict's monastics were known as *cenobites,* a word coming from the Greek *koinos bios,* meaning "common life." Separation from the common life, common prayer, and common meal was a severe discipline applied to correct a wayward monk. The ultimate discipline was separation from the monastery itself (RB 23-25). The community supported its members not only by having them share the work needed for physical survival (RB 66:6) and providing for spiritual nurture and counsel (RB 1:4-5; 3:1-3; 46:5-6; 71-72), but also by giving them time for common prayer, consisting of spoken word followed by silent reflection (RB 19-20). Throughout his Rule, Benedict affirms that the journey is a shared one, "all together to life everlasting" (RB 72:11-12).

The Benedictine tradition calls us to support each other in our shared life of prayer. Later in this book, we will explore more fully the way that practice of common prayer roots Benedictines in the power of Christ's paschal mystery. The community praying the Scriptures together lives out a form of dying and rising with Christ that helps the individual make sense of the rhythms of silence. The daily reading of the psalms, as well as the Passion of Christ, teach that the apparent absence of God is a sure sign of God's love and presence. Over and over Scripture points out that reality is often quite different from appearances: emptiness brings fullness; death channels life; hunger directs toward nourishment. Centered in Scripture and prayer together, the community affirms that apparent negation is a means of freeing us from our always inadequate images of ourselves and God. Silence beyond words teaches the truth and power of the divine, which is utterly other and utterly beyond our capacity to comprehend.

God's own silence is the gift that finally puts us in touch with our deepest desire. Our many desires and needs are refined, purified, transformed into our one great desire: sharing in God's very being. In this utter silence, our hunger and thirst for the only thing which will remedy our partialness is heightened; we accept that we are made for God, and only in the utter vulnerability of naked receptiveness to God do we discover joy and fulfillment. We consent then to give up initiative, fully accepting both our helplessness and our longing. The only thing we can do with assurance is wait. We do nothing, and trust that much is being done, beyond our power to notice. We have not denied our needs, but surrendered them to what surpasses us. In personal blindness, but communal faith, we wait.

5. Accept new life

The final step in active interior silence is to celebrate the changes that God has been working in us. We began with attention to our inner voices, and then sought alternatives to them. Recognizing our limits, we sought God's help, and then realized we must surrender to God in patience. Finally, in this step we notice that God has indeed been active in our waiting, and that new life is already within us. We receive with gladness the changes God has wrought in us, and in gratitude continue to live out our ordinary tasks filled with grace.

Monastic tradition knows silence to be pregnant with creativity. Generations of monastics testify that silence is not the absence of noise, but is the presence of the infinitely creative One whose advent we await with eager longing. Ignatius of Antioch speaks of an "eschatological stillness," a focused waiting in which the end—full participation in God by the whole cosmos—is already present.[11] It is the silence of the Spirit hovering over the waters before creation, the silence after Mary said, "Let it be with me according to your word," in which the one Word of God gestates. It is the silence in which genuine transformation occurs in each beloved child of God in the very moment of apparent nothingness. Renewal takes place in God's time, not ours, and by God's power.

Our task is to maintain the rhythm of word and silence: we speak our need in desire and offering, and then wait for God, expectant and attentive to the new life that emerges in us.

The goal of Benedictine silence is the consecration of all life in the encounter with God. All of life can be welcomed into silence for a moment of meeting with the Holy that penetrates and transforms ordinary experience. Active interior silence creates an environment for listening to God. Benedictines understand listening as Scripture does: it is receiving and responding to what is heard. There is an essential element of change in true listening. In his Rule Benedict gives us an image of deep listening in chapter 5 on obedience:

> They follow by their deeds the voice of the one who commands. And so, as it were at the same instant, the bidding of the master and the perfect work of the disciple are together more perfectly fulfilled in the swiftness of the fear of God. (RB 5:8-9)

This obedience is not compliance; it is obedience in its root sense of deep listening. God empowers what God commands. When we are receptive to the Word of God, a change takes place within us that enables us to experience the wholeness for which we were made. As God draws near in silence and we receive God into our hearts, we are transformed so that we become fully the persons we really are in Christ.

We seldom notice this change while it is happening. Rather, we awake one morning and realize that something is different in us. We are gentler, less frantic and anxious, better able to enjoy small daily gifts, more delighted with others. For each of us, the specific shape of new life takes a slightly different form uniquely suited to our God-given essence. And for each of us, the form taken is so congruent with our longings that we wonder how we were able to manage before the change occurred.

The gifts God bestows are meant for our joy. We have cause for celebration and are enlivened for gratitude. Despite his habitually restrained style, Benedict did not suppress his gladness in the gifts of God. He speaks of "love of Christ, naturally, through a good disposition and delight in virtue" as the fruit of active interior silence (RB 7:70). The gift of new life brings with it delight, manifesting itself in love for Christ everywhere.

Gregory the Great described a moment in the life of Benedict that helps us see what an extraordinary integration of life and prayer is offered by Benedictine spirituality:

> The man of God was standing at his window, where he watched and prayed while the rest were still asleep. In the dead of night he suddenly beheld a flood of light shining down from above more brilliant than the sun, and with it every trace of darkness cleared away. Another remarkable sight followed. According to his own description, the whole world was gathered up before his eyes in what appeared to be a single ray of light.[12]

In the silence of the night, Benedict's soul was so drawn into the mind and light of God that his spirit was enlarged, and he saw anew and welcomed the created world in God's love.

Through the Rule, Benedict invites us to daily practices that can open to us this possibility of living ordinary lives in the fullness of God, alive to the glory thus manifest in us and the world. Persevering in Christ's teachings, by patience we participate in his sufferings, but we will also partake in his kingdom (RB Prologue:50). Silence is a central foundation for such a life.

Endnotes

1. Ambrose G. Wathen, OSB, *Silence: The Meaning of Silence in the Rule of Saint Benedict* (Kalamazoo: Cistercian Studies, 1973), p. 231.

2. The texts on silence in the Rule are chapters 4:52, 6 (entire), 7:56-58, 38:5, and 42 (portions). Adalbert de Vogüé notes: "The whole thing is laconic enough to give the impression of a lesson in taciturnity, as if Benedict wished to join example to teaching" *(The Rule of St. Benedict: A Doctrinal and Spiritual Commentary,* trans. John Baptist Hasbrouck, OCSO [Kalamazoo: Cistercian Publications, 1983], p. 113).

3. Wathen, *Silence,* especially pp. 165-172.

4. de Vogüé, *The Rule,* p. 115.

5. John Cassian, *Conference* VII.3 (Abbot Serenus on Inconstancy of Mind), in Volume XI of *Nicene and Post-Nicene Fathers of the Christian Church,* trans. Edgar C. S. Gibson (Grand Rapids: Eerdmans, 1986), p. 362.

6. Evagrius Ponticus, *Praktikos,* in *The Praktikos and Chapters on Prayer,* trans. John Eudes Bamberger, OCSO (Kalamazoo: Cistercian Publications, 1972), pp. 16-17.

7. Evagrius Ponticus, *Praktikos,* p. 37. Sentence 86 reads in part: "The rational soul operates according to nature when the following conditions are realized: the concupiscible part (that which experiences lust) *desires* virtue" *(my emphasis)*. See also chapter 15 and the conclusion in Louis Bouyer, *The Spirituality of the New Testament and the Fathers* (New York: Seabury, 1982).

8. *The Sayings of the Desert Fathers,* trans. Benedicta Ward, SLG (Kalamazoo: Cistercian Publications and Oxford: A. R. Mowbray, 1975) p. 103.

9. John Cassian, *Conference* IX.28 (The First Conference of Abbot Isaac On Prayer), *Nicene and Post-Nicene Fathers,* Vol. XI, p. 397; and

Gregory of Nyssa, *Oratio* 4, *Contra Julianum* 1; PG35: 593C. An excellent text exploring this monastic vision of the gift of tears is Irénée Hausherr's *Penthos: The Doctrine of Compunction in the Christian East*, trans. Anselm Hufstader, OSB (Kalamazoo: Cistercian Publications, 1982).

10. Bernard of Clairvaux, *Sermon 36.6 on the Song of Songs,* trans. Kilian Walsh, OCSO, vol. 2, Cistercian Fathers Series, 7 (Kalamazoo: Cistercian Publications, 1976), p. 179.

11. Ignatius of Antioch, *Letter to the Ephesians,* XIX.1. Fr. Luke Dysinger, OSB, at St. Andrew's Abbey in Valyermo, California, is the source of the term "eschatological stillness" used to translate Ignatius' term *hesychia*.

12. Gregory the Great, *The Life and Miracles of St. Benedict,* trans. Odo J. Zimmermann, OSB and Benedict R. Avery, OSB (Collegeville, Minn.: The Liturgical Press, 1949), p. 71.

Exercises
in
Silence

One

The next time you can be alone for an extended period, practice complete silence for several hours in a place where you will not be disturbed. Begin exploring the external texture of silence. Can you get a feeling for some taste, touch, and shape which the silence seems to have? (Be playful.) Greet the silence as if it were a person, and listen to it with expectancy. The focus here is on the objective rather than the subjective reality of silence.

Two

Consider practicing silence of several types. Add the silence of body to the silence of tongue: move gently and peacefully, and try to make as little commotion as you can when you walk, sit, and move. Practice silence of mind—including memory and imagination—for as long a period as you can. Often it is helpful to repeat a short prayer phrase to still the mind, like "Lord, have mercy" or "O God, come to my assistance." Finally, add the silence of spirit: hold yourself open in love to the Holy, being content to receive without commenting.

Three

Now try active interior silence. When you are able to set aside an hour or so, clear away all external noises for the specific purpose of attending to inner voices. You might begin by trying to write down every thought you have in fifteen minutes, in an effort to notice any patterns. Is there a theme that keeps recurring? Is there a phrase that appears several times? What are the messages you consistently give yourself?

On another occasion, take the next step of active interior silence. Write out one or two of the main messages you tell yourself on the left side of a large piece of paper. Then write in the right-hand column an alternative statement, based on your trust in God's goodness, power, and love, particularly for you. For example, if the left side says, "You are terribly selfish," on the right side, you might write, "I am to love my neighbor as myself." Then take some time to consider how you are loving yourself as well as your neighbor. How can you strengthen the positive aspects in *both* elements?

When you have finished both of the above steps, review all you have written, and sit back with eyes closed. Seek God's help with what you have written and wait patiently. Offer a prayer of thanksgiving for whatever God will give, before you rise.

Four

When you are doing some routine work for thirty minutes or so, use it as an opportunity to practice silence in the rhythm of your work—whether you are cleaning the house, weeding the garden, or doing heavy manual labor by yourself.

Begin your work with the intention of allowing yourself to be drawn fully into the activity, silencing the chatter of your mind in the rhythm of the labor itself. Whenever your mind tries to catch hold of any project other than the one of your hands, draw it back gently but firmly to the task at hand.

When you have finished, take a few moments to be aware of the inner quiet that has arisen in you.

Five

In a retreat setting, explore the possibility of practicing silence while in the presence of other persons. Notice, whenever you are tempted to speak, what your motives are at the time. Consider alternative means of satisfying those motives; for example, if you want to ask about someone's health, consider praying for him or her instead.

Chapter Two

Holy Reading

The rock sits on a patch of moist earth, reflecting various colors in the bright sun. A slight trickle of water falls from a short distance above, giving the rock a wet sheen in the sunlight. The water is not continuous but intermittent, forming small droplets that gradually fill to the breaking point and release a bit of water onto the rock. Each drop of water falls in exactly the same place. I sit and watch this miracle for several minutes. The rock seems so hard, the water so gentle. Is it possible that in time the persistent drops of water will indeed change the shape of the rock? It seems unlikely. And yet other rocks nearby show clearly the pattern of erosion and transformation caused by years of just such unremitting action. Sometimes things are not as they seem.

In this book we are exploring the elements of Benedictine spirituality, elements that, like the steady, small droplets of living water, have the subtle power to form our being, slowly wearing away the hardness of our rocky hearts. In letting this happen, we are seeking to become more sensitive to the way things really are, and to become more responsive to the gentle and persistent action of divine grace upon our lives.

In chapter 1, we found silence to be a medium for listening to God. In the Hebrew Scriptures, listening or hearing involves responding to what is heard; in the Latin, the verb *ob-audire* (hear toward) means "to obey." A true word has such inherent force that a response is inevitable once we hear it truly. In just such a way was the world created: God's word, spoken forth, called into being a response that it was so! We lack the simplicity of vision and purity of heart to respond so utterly and immediately. For us, to hear and to respond are normally two separate things, cause and effect rather than twin dimensions of a single action.

Benedictine silence involves responding and being transformed as well as listening. Likewise, the monastic practice of *lectio divina*, the prayerful reading of Holy Scripture or spiritual writings, involves hearing as well as response. The chapter on silence emphasized listening; this chapter will focus on response to God as the primary emphasis of the monastic practice of *lectio divina*.

Reflection on the Bible, both in common worship and private prayer, is central to Benedictine life. Benedict asked his followers to spend about four hours each day in the encounter with God in Scripture. The Latin meaning of *lectio divina* is more richly textured than is suggested by its English translation, holy or godly reading. *Lectio* involves a commitment to daily reading, undertaken not primarily as an informational or study project, but as a devotional activity. We read in order to let ourselves be formed, as the rock we spoke of is formed by water. In *lectio* we read not to receive information, for basically we already know what the Bible says. We read to interact with the Word of God; we read to respond to what God offers our life this day.

As so frequently happens in the Rule, the texts giving actual instruction about *lectio* are few and to the point. The main text occurs in the chapter entitled "Daily Manual Labor," in which Benedict noted that "the brethren should be occupied at stated times in manual labor and at other fixed hours in sacred reading *(lectio divina)*" (RB 48:1). He went on to establish a daily schedule in which physical labor and *lectio* vary according to season. In all seasons, the "best" time of the day is set aside for *lectio,* that is, the early morning hours in which the members of the community are fresh, alert, and receptive. During the winter, when crops do not need attention, an additional period of *lectio* is set aside after the midday meal. On Sundays, the whole day is set aside for *lectio* and prayer. Benedict makes it clear that to neglect one's *lectio* is actually to harm oneself (RB 48:18), for although manual labor is required both to exercise, honor, and discipline the body and to support and feed the community, the primary labor of monastics is that of *lectio* and the Divine Office.

Other references to *lectio* in the Rule occur in chapter 4, where it is linked with prayer as one of the "instruments of good works" (RB 4:55-56), and chapter 49, where *lectio* is named as one of the principal gifts ("something beyond the measure appointed") which can be offered to God during Lent. Chapter 8 mentions a special time of study related to *lectio*, emphasizing memorization. Not all early monastics were literate, and very often *lectio* meant recalling passages memorized from hearing Scripture read aloud.

Not all periods set aside for *lectio* are intended for solitary reflection. Indeed, a very high proportion of the total times *lectio* is mentioned in the Rule refers to community gatherings. Throughout the chapters on the Divine Office (community prayer times), references to *lectio* abound. In particular, the earliest office of the day (Vigils) is designed as a "readings" office. *Lectio* provides a way for interaction with Scripture and with God which may be undertaken in community as well as on one's own.

In chapter 38 of the Rule, Benedict also specified that *lectio* shall occur during meals and gave special care to the method of assigning readings and praying with the reader for the week, as well as the attitude the monks are to demonstrate as they listen during meals. Chapter 42 calls for a community gathering just before the final office of the day (Compline) at which *lectio* is also assigned. These two latter assignments apparently refer not to Scripture itself, but to works of the spiritual masters that would be edifying for the community.

Benedict understood *lectio* as an encounter with God, vital to forming the way we live and move and have our being. He knew it to be a radiant source of new life in the person practicing it faithfully. By leading us into the inspired word of God in the Scripture, *lectio* teaches us how to respond to and receive the embrace of the Other who is Creator and Redeemer. This attitude can eventually permeate our view of all life. *Lectio* disposes us to receive the gift of heavenly regard wherever it is offered on any day to any of us.

God's Active Presence in Small Things

Lectio presupposes that God is active and present in our lives, engaging through the Word with each of us in a personal and potentially transforming way. Benedictine spirituality is rooted in the conviction that every passage of Scripture—even the dullest or most obscure—is filled with God and is exactly suited to our life experience at the moment. Indeed, it has been said that Benedict thought of his whole Rule as a practical guidebook for the living out of the gospel message. The Rule seeks to enable us to make Scripture our own, to bring the transforming power of Christ into ordinary experience. Benedict believes that God's Word is living, seeking us out, calling out to us this day, inviting our response.[1] The Word is vitally relevant to the perplexities we encounter in every moment of ordinary life. Every verse of Scripture carries the power to transform our daily experience, not once, but many times.

We can hear these words and have no idea what they might mean in our own lives. For most of us Scripture has provided this healing light at one time or another, but seldom in our routine reading, and almost never at certain passages. In general, we turn to Scripture for historical information or dogmatic reinforcement, but most of us have not experienced a method of Scripture study in which we expect an encounter with the living God, with direct implications for our daily situation.

Four hours a day of reading Scripture seems an incredible investment of time for us moderns, and Benedict's Rule offers no specific instructions for how to "do" *lectio*; it merely sets forth general guidelines, including this astonishing commitment of time. How can reading the Bible cause those life changes to occur that are the essence of following Christ? The elimination of bad habits and selfish ways, the deep shift of heart in which one becomes a truly loving person, the growing docility to the Holy Spirit—how can *lectio* accomplish all these things?

The succinct answer is that in *lectio* we meet the living and powerful God in an encounter that changes us. A ninth-century Benedictine noted that the Rule expects God to be active in our *lectio*, saying: "Someone who wishes to be always with God must pray often and read often. For when we pray, we speak with God, but when we read, God speaks to us."[2] But the succinct answer only raises more questions for us. What does it mean to hear God speak to us? Too often, people who claim to hear God seem actually to be a little strange if not downright crazy! What really happens to ordinary persons like ourselves?

These questions remain unanswerable until we begin a regular practice of *lectio*, discovering for ourselves the unique relationship which will emerge. We can close off real encounter by not doing *lectio* or by doing it superficially. But if we simply give ourselves to the process, in humility and receptivity, *lectio* does its work in our heart. *Lectio* requires a willingness to open the door to God. Generally, God's voice sounds suspiciously like our own. God's word tends to come into our minds regarding the small matters of life that most disturb us. What we receive in *lectio* seems so ordinary that it comes with no surprise, much less with trumpets! We are simply given an insight into the next best thing we can do or be, how we can be true to who we are and to our circumstances. And the answers we receive in the practice of *lectio* will gradually come to infuse our whole attitude toward life. In other words, from the discipline of *lectio* we become so attuned to our relationship with God that it gradually penetrates every aspect of life. Consider a specific example.

Let us say that you are practicing *lectio,* using a passage from Mark 8:2-6, the story of the feeding of the five thousand—well known and often interpreted, though as *lectio* suggests, always new to the responsive heart.

> Jesus said, "I have compassion for the crowd, because they have been with me now for three days, and have nothing to eat. If I send them away hungry to their homes, they will faint on the way—and some of them have come from a great distance." His disciples replied, "How can one feed all these people with bread here in the desert?" He asked them, "How many loaves do you have?" They said, "Seven." Then he ordered the crowd to sit down on the ground; and he took the seven loaves, and after giving thanks he broke them and gave them to his disciples to distribute; and they distributed them to the crowd.

Let us also imagine that this morning your heart is heavy because you argued with your spouse. As you ponder the passage in the light of your unhappiness, you become aware that the phrase of Jesus, "I have compassion for them," seems to draw your attention. You remember that compassion means "to suffer with," and you wonder that Jesus took a body like ours not only that he might know life as we know it, but also that we might know life as God does. You realize that this passage, which is somehow teaching you about your relationship with your spouse, begins with the compassion of Jesus.

And suddenly you see your partner in a whole new light. You realize that he or she is not a powerful person who is depriving you of something, but a fragile, needy person—almost like a child, infinitely precious and vulnerable. You remember your spouse's delight in life, as well as his or her occasional weariness. With this, all the momentum is taken out of your anger, and it is no longer important to claim your rights against your partner. Instead, you want to comfort and help.

But you realize that you cannot do even that, because you don't have the necessary resources. You yourself are in the desert. How can you feed someone? And you turn to ask this question of Jesus, only to find him asking you: What *do* you have? He seems to be asking you to look carefully and realistically at what you actually have. You do that, and then bring those resources to Jesus. And he surprises you.

Jesus first asks you to rest and sit down. Then he takes what you have brought and gives thanks. He is always aware that everything comes from God, and in the gospels he frequently gives thanks for what he offers to God. However small or unimpressive it seems, he praises

God for his unlimited abundance. Then, he breaks it. He breaks you. He splits apart the resources you have—your expectations, your rights, your pride, your control, even your gifts. He shows you how much your own expectations get in the way of your seeing clearly. But in the breaking, he also shows you—even more astonishingly— how profoundly your own needs provide exactly the resource he can use. He shows you that your brokenness is his gift. Your incapacity is exactly the opening through which God's grace and power can flow. And now you rest in his love.

Your own periods of *lectio* may be longer or shorter than this example suggests. They may be more narrowly or more broadly focused. But they will in all probability be formed by the truth of the Scriptures and tradition and will be immediately relevant to your own life experience in just this way. You may find at first that you only remember for a few moments afterwards to act upon what you have understood, so quickly do you return to your "old ways." But if you stay with *lectio,* you will discover that you are growing more and more into the mind and heart of Christ, and surprising yourself with major shifts in disposition as you do.

Because this process is so personal, it will vary from time to time with any one person, and it will vary greatly among individuals. At first, *lectio* may seem laborious and unrewarding, and we may wonder whether we are simply playing psychological games with ourselves. As always, the soundness of any spiritual discipline is discovered in its fruits: have I become kinder, gentler, more patient and loving with myself and others? Am I contributing to the common good? Here a spiritual director or a discerning friend can help guide us. But *lectio* requires us to take seriously the Scriptures of our faith;

over time, the content of these Scriptures itself begins to mold the way we think and act. At first, the interaction between life and Scripture may be shaped primarily by our own attitudes and predispositions. Later, as we deepen in maturity and receptivity to what we read, the text itself takes more of the shaping role. Our dispositions will be changed by the Word of God in Scripture.

Perhaps this assurance of the growing importance of the text in guiding our lives will still be a source of concern to some of us. After all, there is a great deal of material in the Bible, some of it not very edifying and most of it subject to a wide variety of interpretation. When we say that the text begins to shape us, have we in fact said something positive?

Many Layers of Meaning

Our concern with the content of Scripture comes in large part from our modern scholarly approach to the Bible. We tend to read exclusively on the historical-critical level—what the ancients called the "literal" or "historical" level of Scripture. Although few of us would insist that the Bible literally means that the world was created in six days, many of us have been trained to approach the Bible for the "facts" there. We search for the historical record and confine our attention to the intellectual content. We are concerned to find the right meaning of any specific passage, and we look to experts to guide us in discovering that meaning. We are always asking the question, Did this actually happen?, by which we mean, Is this historically true? At some level, we are aware that this approach is a narrowing of the traditional approach of Christians to Scripture, but we are not sure how to read it any other way.

The Benedictine discipline of *lectio* is rooted in what is known as the "allegorical" method of scriptural exegesis, which includes several levels of interpretation at once. According to this ancient method, the reader searches for four different meanings in every text. The first meaning is the *literal* or *historical* meaning, which is followed by three kinds of "spiritual" meanings. The *allegorical* finds Christ in the text. This exploration is founded in the conviction that Christ is so inherent in the structure of the universe—and particularly in sacred Scripture—that everything speaks of him. All specific passages will be a type, or an allegory, of the reality of Christ's presence, and our spiritual work begins by seeking him in the passage. The *tropological* finds the moral or behavioral implications in the text. Here the spiritual seeker is searching for a guide or directive for Christian action in the specific passage. The *anagogical* finds eternal or ultimate meaning in the text. The reader searches for the way the text reveals God's ultimate purposes breaking through into history.

John Cassian spoke of the integrated spiritual knowledge to be found in Scripture, giving the simple example of the image of the city of Jerusalem in which all four meanings can coalesce:

> One and the same Jerusalem can be taken in four senses; historically, as the city of the Jews, allegorically as the Church of Christ, analogically as the heavenly city of God "which is the mother of us all," tropologically as the soul of man, which is frequently subject to praise or blame from the Lord under this title.[3]

This way of reading Scripture was also used by such notable early Christians as Hilary, Ambrose, and Augustine of Hippo, and was the principal method used not only by Benedict himself, but also by Benedictines throughout the Middle Ages. It was largely abandoned by systematic theologians and by reformers, when new modes of scholarship concentrated on the historical meaning. A reconsideration of this older method helps us as we turn to Scripture with the primary desire of responding to God there. *Lectio* profits greatly from the advances of contemporary scholarship, but depends upon the ancient, more symbolic mode of reading.

Benedict himself gives an example in the Rule of how this four-part method of Scripture reading can open a difficult text. In the Prologue, Benedict wrote of

> one who has brought the malignant devil to naught, casting him out of the sight of his heart with all his sug- gestions; and has taken hold of his bad thoughts, while they were still young, and dashed them down upon Christ. (RB Prologue:28)

This passage includes a quotation from Psalm 137:9, in which the Israelite psalmist praised those who dashed Babylonian babies on the rocks before they had a chance to grow up and become oppressors like their fathers. Benedict was so enchanted with this verse from the psalms that he alludes to it again later in the Rule:

> Dash down at the feet of Christ all your evil thoughts, the instant that they come into your heart; and lay them open to your spiritual father. (RB 4:50)

Benedict was able to understand this passage from the psalms, so repugnant to modern ears that it is generally omitted from contemporary lectionaries, as divinely in- spired and edifying to him personally. In part he was able to do so because he was applying a key principle of *lectio,* that of being willing to enter his own discomfort and stay with it in his conviction that God was present and would bring transformation. Benedict was also able to do so because he identified the rock with Christ, using a method of Scripture reading that enabled him to discover deeper riches underneath the horror of the literal meaning of the text.

Benedict's interpretation of the spiritual meaning of the passage does not have three distinct parts, with one for each kind of meaning. Rather, the three meanings are intertwined. By *allegorical* application, the "rock" is Christ, the unshakable foundation of the faith of his disciples. By the *moral* meaning, temptations are to be dashed against that rock in their infancy, that is, they are to be immediately offered to Christ before they gain a foothold in our hearts. The *anagogical* meaning is that because we have already been redeemed from our sins, we are fully able to deal with the temptations which still arise, because we put our trust in Christ.

By this example, we can see how these three interrelated spiritual meanings can be applied to our own Scripture reading.

At the allegorical level, we see Christ present here and now, in that part of the created world which is given to each of us this day. We have a keen sense that we are not alone; we are met and touched in our present need. Our daily experience is gently enfolded by the Word present in Scripture.

At the tropological or moral level, we discern the ethical and practical implications of our actions which are consequent on the discovery of Christ here and now. We realize that we do have choices, often newly or redemptively seen. Our situation is highlighted by the presence of Christ so that suddenly what we thought were the dust and ashes of our life are seen as gems:

Christ is in their midst in a very particular way, and because of this we are not only invited but empowered to adopt new behavior.

At the anagogical level, we experience a growing awareness that the present time is not sharply separated from eternity. The intimacy with Christ discovered in the Scripture moves us forward beyond time, so that we glimpse heavenly realities. Our present life is shaped not only by the past, but also by God's empowerment of who we are called to become. Our part in God's eternal plan is somehow an invitation to us in our present setting. We are urged to open ourselves to the power of God for healing and wholeness implicit in the moment at hand.

These levels of meaning are often more *experienced* than articulated in words. *Lectio* touches us in the depths of our being, but does not necessarily show itself in logical thoughts during the reading itself. The heart and the will are gradually changed and transformed in *lectio*, so that in time all of life begins to seem new. But this is slow and not necessarily conscious, though it requires our willingness.

The basis of *lectio* and the allegorical method is the pattern of listening, response, and transformation. *Lectio* draws the reader ever more deeply into the encounter with Christ, which has concrete application in our life in a way that also transcends time. The key elements of *lectio*'s response are illumined in the allegorical method, and they include: seeing Christ in the midst of life experiences; making concrete choices and receiving the necessary strength to act; and living in the sense of hope and invitation born from the glimpse of eternity breaking through into time. *Lectio* and the allegorical approach to Scripture teach us a foundational approach to

Scripture and life, inviting us to respond faithfully to God in our midst.

Rumination

A homely metaphor for *lectio divina* often used by medieval spiritual guides is "rumination." A cow ruminates as she chews and digests her food. Actually, the noun "ruminant" applies to a number of animals who share the characteristics of a second stomach, cloven-hooved feet, horns, and a diet of grasses and foliage; it includes oxen, sheep, goats, antelopes, giraffes, and deer, as well as cattle. Rumination does not seem to tell us much about what *lectio* is, except perhaps that it is the careful rechewing of otherwise indigestible material! Yet as we explore the metaphor, we discover many likenesses that help us understand *lectio* better.

Most ruminants, unlike the familiar cow, tend to be adapted for swift flight, and although they have horns, they almost never use them against their enemies, except when cornered. Good grazing lands tend to be full of natural enemies of the ruminants. Therefore, these animals are extremely well adapted for snatching a meal hastily in a favorable place and then storing the food temporarily in a special compartment of their stomach until they have found a quiet and safe haven to digest it at leisure. Immediately, we sense a parallel with the idea of rumination in our Scripture reading. Perhaps we have only a short period in which to read a passage of Scripture, but we can store it away for further reflection. At a later time we return to seek essential nourishment from the hastily gathered passage.

The other major focus of this metaphor is the material being chewed. A ruminant begins with hard grasses and coarse foliage, which are not easily digestible, and ends with protein-rich milk. What an astonishing transformation! How does it occur? We tend to take such ordinary miracles for granted. We do not, perhaps, feel an equal ease with the transformation that occurs in *lectio,* the transformation of a puzzling Scripture passage or a conflict-filled event into those responses that cumulatively produce sainthood. All the cow does to produce this wonder of milk is chew her cud. When she finds a place of safety, she lies down and waits a while. A small spasm, like a hiccough, signals that a bolus of grass has been returned from the first stomach and is ready to be chewed. Patiently the animal chews away, first on one side, then on the other, until the grass has been reduced to a pulp and can go back to the stomach for final chemical digestion.

Just as the cow must chew her cud to produce milk, so we must sit quietly for a time, patient and waiting, enjoying the safety. We are given something that presses itself on our attention: a phrase from Scripture or a moment from the day. We turn our attention to it, looking at it from this way and that. We bring our minds and our emotions and our life experiences to it; we also are deliberately aware of the presence of God in the midst of it all. And having done what we can, we turn it over to the natural processes of our spirit. We give it back to God and go on with life. This is rumination. This is the *lectio* response to God which Benedict teaches.

A Pattern for Our Lives

Many of us are hungry for a pattern of discipline by which we may regularly and faithfully respond to God's communication to us. We want to try *lectio*. But how? We need more than Benedict's admonition that we do it for four hours a day! If we endeavor to draw from all these examples a simple procedure by which we could practice *lectio* as part of our own daily spiritual discipline, how might we go about it?

Perhaps we can discern a method from Scripture itself. Luke's gospel offers an example of *lectio* at its best in the story of the Annunciation. This is the passage:

> In the sixth month the angel Gabriel was sent by God to a town in Galilee called Nazareth, to a virgin engaged to a man whose name was Joseph, of the house of David. The virgin's name was Mary. And he came to her and said, "Greetings, favored one! The Lord is with you." But she was much perplexed by his words and pondered what sort of greeting this might be. The angel said to her, "Do not be afraid, Mary, for you have found favor with God. And now, you will conceive in your womb and bear a son, and you will name him Jesus."...
>
> Mary said to the angel, "How can this be, since I am a virgin?"
>
> The angel said to her, "The Holy Spirit will come upon you, and the power of the Most High will overshadow you; therefore the child to be born will be holy; he will be called the Son of God....For nothing will be impossible with God."
>
> Then Mary said, "Here I am, the servant of the Lord; let it be with me according to your word." Then the angel departed from her. (Luke 1:26-38)

From the point of view of someone seeking to understand *lectio,* what is happening here? First, we can assume some *preparation*. Mary is a devout young woman, steeped in the Hebrew Scriptures, faithful in ordinary religious practice, and taking it all to heart. In works of art, Mary is often shown as reading when the angel appears, suggesting the intense concentration and application characteristic of *lectio.* Her faith excites her and stirs her soul, and she believes that it will dramatically affect her life and that of her people, though she cannot imagine quite how.

Second, there is an opportunity to *hear*. Gabriel appears to Mary and she listens to his word to her. One phrase particularly attracts her ("favored one"), and she ponders it over and over in her heart.

Third, there is *touch*. Mary explores with her mind the meaning of what she has heard, wondering how it is going to affect her. As Mary ponders what she has heard in the light of what she already knows, the import of this word on her life becomes clear: God is asking her to carry a child who will be the Savior. The meaning she discovers may not make complete sense to her and she does not yet understand its full implications, but she is deeply touched by it. She realizes her own vulnerability, the cost to her standing in her community and the possible effect on her impending marriage. She asks the question to which she must know the answer: "How can this be?" She turns over the word, asking how her life will be touched by it.

Fourth, there is *invitation*. As Mary applies what she has understood to her own life, to her feelings and longings, she realizes that God's touch carries an implicit question to her: will she consent to cooperate in this essential creative work? The kingdom of God has drawn so near to her in this moment that, if she consents, nothing will ever be the same again. God waits for her response: she understands that the question which only she can answer is now addressed to her. "Mary, will you be my mother?"

Fifth, there is *response*. Mary accepts and savors what she has received. Satisfied and filled by Gabriel's answer, Mary responds in love: "Let it be with me according to your word." And she is transformed. The fruit will appear only later, in stages: the praise of the *Magnificat,* the birth of Jesus, her perseverance from the foot of the cross to the upper room at Pentecost. Mary was so receptive to the Word of God that she conceived him in her womb. Mary models in a unique way the call each Christian receives to accept and nurture God's very life so that new birth happens in us, as the essence and the call of *lectio,* the meditative art of Benedict.

Let us, then, draw on Mary's experience to see what we can discover about how to practice *lectio* ourselves. Let us review her process. First, she prepared. How can we *prepare* for *lectio?* We come as we are, not as we wish we were. We bring our full life experience; we are present now just as we are. A regular rhythm of personal prayer and community worship and familiarity with the Bible all help us to be receptive to what we may encounter. As we come to read, we must be simply who and what we are at this moment. And we must be *here,* attentive, and not mentally somewhere else. We take a moment always at the beginning of *lectio* to quiet down, to make the shift from whatever has been going on, to recollect ourselves to God's presence in this moment. First, we prepare.

Second, we *hear.* We come to our *lectio* time with expectancy that we will encounter God, and we are attentive to what we hear, listening carefully for a word or phrase from the Scripture passage that seems particularly to draw our attention. We take the phrase that especially comes to us, and repeat it over and over, even with our lips, letting our bodies hear it too. We listen with the ear of our hearts, hearing the word addressed to each of us.

Third, we ask, how am I *touched* by this word? Having received a word or a phrase, we ponder it. We reflect on it, turning it over and over, asking what it means, what it says to us today. We engage the passage with our minds, asking what implications the phrase has for our lives today. We relate whatever is going on in our lives to the word, asking what it says to us in our situation. We may need to ask a question, or to seek clarification, though we do not expect to understand fully yet. We also engage our emotions, noting any feelings that surface, such as peacefulness or reluctance. Sometimes it is helpful to allow a sensory "touch," an image or a sound, to suggest itself as a way of exploring the meaning of the word we have received. We explore how our lives are touched by this word.

Fourth, we receive its *invitation*. We ask what implications the phrase has for our lives today. What is God asking of us or offering to us with this word? Is there some response God seeks from us? The invitation may lead to some radical or long-term life change, but the focus of the moment is on the near term. Is there something small we feel drawn to do or to be in response to what we have heard? Acknowledging that any invitation potentially changes us, we need to ask what we are willing to offer. We receive an invitation to renewed lives by this word.

Fifth, we *respond*. We savor whatever has happened. We allow the fire of God to penetrate and warm our hearts. We abide in God's life, receiving the gift God is offering us, the gift of God's very self, and let ourselves be transformed by this encounter. We receive, responding as we have been empowered.

Five simple steps have been revealed in the example of *lectio* gleaned from Mary's experience of God in Scripture:

1. Prepare
2. Hear (read)
3. Ask how life is touched

4. Receive an invitation
5. Respond and be transformed

These steps can be considered as very roughly parallel to the elements we discovered in the allegorical approach to the Bible. Preparation is the same in both. Through hearing we discern a literal meaning, while being touched brings us to the allegorical meaning: Christ is here! Receiving an invitation suggests the anagogical meaning: the future penetrates the present. And responding in prayer and life is the moral meaning: let me be empowered to be God's person in this moment. In all five of these elements, we continue to be aware of the response created within and invited from us: attentiveness to what is, seeing Christ here, experiencing hope, and making choices in daily life.

Lectio-on-Life

The response that begins to be habitual as we practice *lectio* over time will spill over into other arenas of our lives. As we turn to Scripture in expectancy of a living encounter with God, we will begin to wonder if God meets us in the same empowering and transforming way in other settings as well. Might we trust that it is God's desire to be active and present, speaking to each of us in a personal and potentially transforming way in our daily life?

The art of receiving God in everything begins with Scripture, where we have discovered a method of response. After all, we believe that the Bible is inspired and thus a reliable lens through which to understand God's action in our lives. Yet from the moment we first encountered *lectio,* we have realized that this receptive attention is intended not only for Scripture, but also for personal experience. So far this interaction between *lectio* and life has chiefly been illustrated by bringing life questions to texts of Holy Scripture. But dare we start with the text of life itself? Dare we try to "read" our own life situations by the method of *lectio,* with expectancy that we will potentially discover there the kind of vital power, guidance, and nourishment that reward the attentive focus of *lectio* in Scripture?

One of the great surprises that accompanies regular *lectio* is the delightful and awe-inspiring fact that God *does* await us there, with a "word" just for our need at this moment. The word we receive may be very small, yet it somehow brings with it a sense of challenge, strength, and hope. Gradually we come to trust that if God is faithful and present in every small bit of Scripture (which God inspired), God will be as faithful and present in every moment of life (which God created and sustains). We come to an unshakable conviction that every small or large moment, every remote or public place, belongs to God, that *everywhere* God is present to love and to enable us.

Lectio-on-life begins with a gentle and gradual attentiveness to the events of our day in the conviction that God is there, applying the method of *lectio divina* to our personal salvation history, which is unfolding in this moment and this situation. Lectio-on-life is prayerful attention to our own life events as if they, too, are a sacred text.

In the second chapter of the Gospel of Luke, Luke twice tells us that Mary "kept all these things in her heart." The events of Mary's life called her to rumination. What were these events? In Luke 2:19 the shepherds burst into the stable where Mary and Joseph were staying with the newborn infant Jesus, praising God that the Savior Christ had been born. This incident is so familiar to us that we perhaps forget the impact of these events on Mary. After her meeting with the angel Gabriel, Mary must surely have gone through an intense period of pain and trial. Joseph threatened not to marry her, and although he changed his mind, both must have suffered a great anguish of doubt. She had to leave her tiny village (what would the neighbors think?) and go away to her cousin Elizabeth, to live privately while her belly swelled. Yet Mary did not have the support of Elizabeth's presence at the time of Jesus' birth; instead, the young and vulnerable woman had to ride on a donkey for days to a strange city, where she was unable to find decent accommodations, and she gave birth in the discomfort of a stable, surrounded by animals. What must she have thought?

Mary was likely tempted in one of two ways. She might have suspected either that she had misunderstood the message from the angel and all this was a terrible mockery, or she might have insisted on believing that Jesus was going to be the King of Israel despite all the factual evidence which seemed to point to the contrary. She must have wanted the comfort of one clear view or the other, rather than to continue living with the apparent paradox of what her faith suggested and what events revealed. The shepherds' message could not relieve the turmoil, but in a certain sense could only make it worse. Shepherds were among the poorest and most marginal members of Palestinian society—handling animals and hides was almost unclean work—and why should the Lord of heaven and earth announce such an earthshaking event to them, of all people? In the face of all this, Mary pondered.

From the point of view of *lectio*-on-life, what is happening here? First, life happens. An incident occurs. If we are prepared to discover in life more than meets the eye because of what our *lectio* with Scripture has taught us, we recognize the action of God in simple everyday events: relationships, encounters, memories, dreams. Something seems just to happen, but its nature suggests that it has been specially given. The shepherds came to the cave, and Mary—who had expected this moment of birth to be momentously important because of her inner preparation—found that the actual event was quite ordinary, even disappointing. She acknowledged its importance anyway; she received the incident as given by God.

Second, we attend to what has been given. At a later time when we are not rushing on to the next moment, we consciously allow ourselves to bring an incident back into our memory because it suggests a fullness that we may have missed the first time. We hear it again and are gently present to it, paying closer attention. We hear. Mary pondered this event in her heart. She chose to come back to it and pore over it for whatever it might offer.

Third, we allow ourselves to be touched by the incident. We recall it in memory, trying to be as faithful to what actually happened as we can, reconstructing the occurrence with as many of its sensations as possible. What did we see, and what did we hear, smell, taste, and touch? What actually happened? We can also recreate the emotional impact of the incident: where was the most intense energy? Was there a moment of marked change in energy levels? As we undertake this step, we are also attentive to inner resonances—not only what was happening externally and internally at the time, but also how we might be aware of Christ's presence in the event, both then and now. Perhaps one image or phrase comes to us that somehow summarizes our whole experience. We are touched.

Mary surely recalled every detail of the shepherds' visit. She remembered the coarse clothes they wore, and the smell of sheep that hung about them. She remembered the feel of the harsh straw on which she lay, a welcome protection from the cold. She remembered the sound of the cattle lowing and the stridency of the shepherds' voices. She recreated it all in her mind. And she remembered her emotions: the shock at having visitors, and her initial reluctance to allow the dirty men into her birth room. She remembered how tired she had felt, and yet how happy. She remembered the feeling of warmth and comfort her tiny son brought her as he lay close to her breast. She recalled Joseph's effort to protect her and his evident bewilderment at so many strange events. And as she remembered all these feelings, she realized that they reached a peak when one of the quieter young shepherds had looked full at her and said with such awe and assurance: "God sent us here. The angels said we'd never see anything like this again in our whole lives. And I'm glad I came." Her heart turned over when he said that, and a moment later the phrase from the psalm came into her mind, and repeated itself over and over: "The Lord is my shepherd; I shall not want."

Fourth, in *lectio*-on-life, we wonder how to respond to the invitation in the incident itself. An invitation has a give-and-take quality. We begin with an awareness that the event was in some sense "given," and we close with an intentional return of the incident to the Giver. We offer the whole thing back to God—as unresolved, frustrating, or satisfying. We now take the step of releasing everything to God, acknowledging the union of the incident and God's presence in it by offering everything back to God. And then we are silent, waiting, open. We rest in and wait for God, content to receive without comment whatever has been and is being given. In the silence, we may gradually receive a sense that some invitation is being extended to us about the next few days. It may be simply that we feel more lighthearted about our burdens; we may receive an apparently random idea about something we would like to do. There is invitation.

Remembering that incident a few months later, Mary would have smiled to herself at the incongruity of thinking about a particular young, barely-bearded, solemn-eyed young man (who was, it is true, a shepherd) in the same instant as the Lord of all heaven and earth! Yet that silly mismatch had given her great comfort at the time; somehow it seemed to bridge the gulf between what she had imagined and what actually happened on that birth day. Now she gives a great sigh, and offers up all her thoughts to God, resting for a moment in the cool shade and watching a bird in a nearby bush. She glances over at the baby lying at her side, and Jesus seems to give her such a serious look that impulsively she hugs him to her, and coos: "I know you are special, little one! I won't forget!"

Finally, in *lectio*-on-life we respond. Often the boundary between this step and the fourth is blurred: the invitation is received and we respond. Usually the form of the invitation occurs so naturally in the flow of our thoughts that our response seems quite ordinary and almost automatic. But it helps to recall both that we always have a choice—we are always free to accept or refuse—and that when we do choose God, we are always aided by the Holy Spirit with resources beyond our strength. The first moment of response is often only the beginning of an unfolding reality we cannot then imagine. So we go on with our lives, taking the next best step we can.

Here, for *lectio*-on-life, we again have five simple steps, corresponding to those of *lectio* itself:

1. Life happens.
2. We recall an incident attentively. We hear.
3. We ponder what has occurred, seeking God. We are touched by the Word.
4. We offer the incident to God, receptive to invitation.
5. We respond, empowered to go on in a new way.

The same underlying pattern continues throughout this chapter: attentiveness to what is, seeing Christ here, experiencing hope for emerging new life, and making choices in our daily life.

As Mary pondered, she did not immediately try to resolve the tension between her faith and the events. Instead, she consented to accept both fully. She continued to believe that the visitation from Gabriel was of incomparable importance, but she accepted that the way things were going to work out was not as she envisaged. Her son would be the Savior, but she could not even imagine what that would mean. She consented to continue to struggle with these paradoxes and with God, willing not to understand fully, willing to appear foolish, willing to suffer inward doubt, willing still to be God's handmaid in whatever way she could each day.

The apparent simplicity of *lectio*-on-life may mask for us the extraordinary power of transformation implicit in dealing reverently with our life experiences in the expectation that God is always revealed there. In *lectio*-on-life we respond to God, we open ourselves to becoming our real selves, the "not-yet" which God knows in us even when we do not. In *lectio*-on-life we are tapping into that holiness in which our lives are enfolded.

In her reflection on life's events, Mary continued to ponder the circumstances of her life, not in fantasy but in reality, aware that in some unique way God was meeting her there. She sought always to be a fit partner in God's purpose for her. We could say that Mary modeled a process which Benedict adopted: four hours of daily *lectio* naturally involves some reflection on life, as the reader ponders specific paradoxes which occur in every life and allows them to form that interior humility so central to Benedictine spirituality and so necessary to the service of God.

Have we wandered a long way from the teachings of Benedict here? Certainly we have no evidence that Benedict ever pondered these particular passages concerning Mary as he developed his method of *lectio*. Yet these examples may serve to deepen our appreciation of the relevance of this ancient art to our own lives, and send us back with new eyes to observe in the Rule various elements we had previously neglected. Some commentators have wondered why so many chapters of the Rule are devoted to the daily practice of ordinary life. Yet as we begin to consider what *lectio* might mean for us, it seems only natural to think that Benedict would have applied his deeply integrating art of *lectio* to all of Scripture and to all the experiences of his life.

It is no surprise, therefore, to find near the very end of the Rule a chapter that reveals for us a life deeply transformed by the art of *lectio*. In chapter 66—thought to be the original ending of the Rule—we meet the porter of the monastery, the doorman who is assigned to greet all visitors. He is someone prepared by life and age to notice whatever appears at the gate. We might envision him as listening attentively for any knock or call, knowing that all guests are to be received as Christ. So imbued with the pattern of seeing Christ in all and finding hope there, the porter is able to seek the blessing of the stranger. "With all gentleness in the fear of God, he is to answer [anyone] quickly in the fervor of love" (RB 66:4). The stranger is greeted as someone who is a blessing to all who encounter him or her. Invitation and response have become so entwined in the life of the porter that his hope is never disappointed, because he receives the nourishment and embrace of God in everything, even the stranger at the door.

Endnotes

1. All of these verbs occur in the Prologue of the Rule of Saint Benedict, verses 8-20.

2. Smaragdus, *Commentary on the Rule*, 4.56, in *The Sayings of the Fathers*, 102:784. Smaragdus (d. 824) was the abbot of St. Mikiel, Verdun.

3. Cassian, *Conference* XIV.8 (Abbot Nesteros on Spiritual Knowledge), in *Nicene and Post-Nicene Fathers*, Vol. XI, p. 438.

Exercises in Holy Reading

One

Take up one book of the Bible, perhaps starting with the Gospel of Mark. Set aside about twenty minutes each day for *lectio* with that book. Read until a word or phrase attracts your attention. Then (even if you have read less than a verse), lay aside the book, and follow the pattern of *lectio divina* suggested in this chapter. Repeat the single phrase over and over until you really *hear* it. Then consider how it *touches* you today. Is there an *invitation* here for you? *Respond* as seems best now.

If it takes many months to go through the entire book, do not worry, but just be with God as you read.

Two

Reread a favorite story in Scripture, and then imagine what the event might have been like for the protagonists if they had "pondered" it as Mary did. For example, consider the story of Peter walking on the water (Matt. 14:22-33). If you find it helpful, recreate the sensory elements of the scene. Then imagine the emotional shifts. As you consider what it might have been like, ask yourself whether there is an invitation here for your response today.

Three

When you encounter a passage of Scripture which seems especially difficult or confusing to you, apply to it the fourfold allegorical method of interpretation. First, determine the literal or historical meaning, as you understand it. Then ask, is there an allegory or type of Christ here? What implications are there for your behavior? Is there a way you can sense God's long-range purposes manifesting themselves through the passage?

Four

Try practicing *lectio* or *lectio*-on-life with a small group of fellow Christians.* You may find that your common purpose helps everyone to listen more attentively. If you wish to share, do so briefly.

---

* For more direction on *lectio* in groups, consult my book *Bible Reading for Spiritual Growth* (San Francisco: Harper Collins, 1993), which gives practical tips and provides the fictional illustration of a small group of people practicing *lectio* together for a year.

Chapter Three

Prayer

W hy do we pray? When we kneel in church or at the bedside, or send an unspoken petition as an ambulance passes, or cry out to God in anguish, or delight in a sunrise, what are we doing? We are engaging in conversation. We are asking for something or expressing gratitude or praise; we are communicating with Someone not tangible yet vital to us. And at its best, conversation is oriented toward some sort of union. Two friends converse to share ideas or events important to them. Beneath our requests or our thanksgivings in prayer is a wish to be drawn into the divine life. We long to abide with God and to know that God abides with us. We want the wholeness that comes from finding our rest in God and from extending that wholeness into our experience of the world. We long to be drawn into God's very being. We desire to love the Lord God and our neighbor as ourselves, and to reconcile the world to God in Christ.

In our spiritual life, we seek to hear and respond to God, and yet we seek still more than that. We desire to be transformed. We hope to bring to our experience of the world in which we live that abundant life which only comes when God is near. We hear the beautiful words of promise from our tradition and Scripture; we respond as best we can; and we anticipate the promised presence of God in our lives. We worship and pray because God deserves our worship, but also because we want something.

If this definition of prayer sounds shockingly self-serving, consider the language of the Gospel of Matthew, in which Jesus promises that those who follow his teachings will have their reward (Matt. 6:1ff.). This language is also very much a part of Benedict's thought, suggesting as he does that God will reward the service of the faithful (RB 4:76-77; 5:18-19; 20:1-2).

Do we acknowledge that we want something from God? Do we believe it better to worship and pray without desire—indifferent to the outcome? Sometimes we hear religious language that we interpret as requiring detachment and willingness to take whatever comes. Yet we do a disservice to God and ourselves if we apply such an instruction too broadly. It is true that when we pray we are seeking to surrender ourselves to God and God's will, but it is also true that when we pray we are seeking a relationship that will make a fundamental difference in our lives. We are made in God's image precisely for that relationship, and God has placed a longing in our hearts that makes us restless and unsatisfied in the absence of that loving unity. This deepening relationship with God is like falling in love: everything becomes new and wonderful because of this loving. My life and living itself have a sense of wholeness that cannot be imagined outside a loving unity. It is right and good to long for the ineffable and to seek actually to live in the fullness of the unbounded; we were made for this.

What does such language mean? Take a few moments right now and ask yourself: what is the quality of my life today? Each of us will have a unique response, but there will likely be some similarities, because we share a common time and space. Each day I go about my duties and responsibilities, finding more or less satisfaction in their accomplishment. I read the newspaper, watch television, and wonder about the terrible problems of poverty, violence, greed, dishonesty, and isolation that beset our world. Sometimes I do a little something to help. I worship in a local community that has some sense of mutuality. I live with my own body and its needs, taking some care of it and perhaps giving in to some of its compulsions, depending upon my particular temperament. I have some family, some friends, and some acquaintances who gather occasionally for shared pleasures. There is some mix of happiness and sadness, delight and grief, in my life, as in every life.

But where are the places that require my greatest energy? What are the issues I find my baffled mind returning to again and again? Which problems cause my stomach to be upset most often? In every life, there are troublesome elements, elements with which we struggle day in and day out, seemingly making no progress. Maybe it is an addiction to cigarettes, which our friends consider vile and which we secretly know causes our bodies harm. Maybe it is a difficult older parent living with us who is never pleased by anything we do, or an adult child who has run away from home and refuses any contact. Maybe it is a work setting in which we feel constantly pressured to compromise our values. Maybe it is a concern for the poor, which evokes in us a nagging sense of guilt we cannot release. Maybe it is a subtle dissatisfaction we cannot really name but that makes us feel somehow that our life is incomplete.

Each life has its serious struggles and burdens, and we somehow expect that a growing relationship of love with the all-powerful God will make a difference in areas of our pain and grief and restlessness. We want real transformation in the midst of life, not pie-in-the-sky-when-we-die. And such hope is congruent with the promise of the gospel, for this is the promise: "If anyone is in Christ, there is a new creation" (2 Cor 5:17). With Christ, everything becomes new. Transformation has been brought about and can come about in our very being in this broken world. Through baptism, we are one body with him; Christ abides in us, drawing all things into their intended fullness in himself. Scripture and tradition tell us that somehow through Christ, God has burst the limitations of our lives, bestowing that fullness for which we deeply long. We pray for the coming of God's kingdom, knowing that it is already here waiting to fill both our inner and outer realities with justice and peace. Why then do we experience brokenness instead of abundance? Why do we continue to have this inner disquiet? Why are we not able to live as we sense we are intended to live? If we have heard aright, why don't we know it? Can we trust the promise of God in Christ? Does transformation really happen in ordinary people's lives?

These are the longings and questions of prayer. We want God to make a difference—we need a new creation! As we enter fully into the spiritual journey, we become acutely aware of our own helplessness. To create the good, abundant life is beyond our capacities. Something in us is made for this abundance; something in us inevitably obscures it. We seek something more satisfying than we can ask or imagine but we cannot provide it, so we turn to God in prayer, asking to be filled with the gift promised in Christ's life. For, if there is any hope of transformation, it must lie in this mutual indwelling with God which Christ models and offers us. This relationship of loving union is the only possible way for us to be what we want to be, to live as we believe we were meant to live. And it is our desire for transformation that keeps us seeking such union: life must be more than this! As a sign of your abiding life, O God, give us that transformation for which we long.

Chronos and Kairos

A phrase often used to express this longing for what is never fully experienced in our lives is "already and not yet." The kingdom of God has already broken into the world in Christ's death and resurrection, but everything has not yet been drawn into it. The grace of God has already been given in fullness, and we are not yet able to receive it as fully as we could. Christ is all in all, but the union of all things in him is yet to come. Something exists in the present that has not yet come to be. This is indeed mysterious language for those who understand time as measured and fixed.

Christian Scripture and tradition refer to two different kinds of time. The Greek word *chronos* refers to time experienced as duration, as chronological progression and continuity. That this concept of time dominates our contemporary views is suggested by its many cognates in English. A chronicle is a record, a chronometer is a clock, a chronic condition is one of long duration.

Theologically, the more important Greek word for time is *kairos,* referring to a time of opportunity, of special potential or heightened readiness. When Jesus says, "The time is near!" (Luke 21:8), he is speaking of *kairos.*[1] The word *kairos* expresses the transforming power of God's presence within human history, made fully tangible in the life of Jesus Christ of Nazareth. *Kairos* suggests the presence of the fullness of God in a way that unites past, present, and future and points toward their fulfillment. *Kairos* expresses the truth that the incarnation of God's transforming power is in our midst now. The life of Jesus Christ embodies such transforming power and promises its presence in our lives as well, yet this New Testament word for time transformed has produced no contemporary English cognates.

Paying attention to time as *kairos* enables us humans to become channels by which the power of the future shapes the present. *Kairos* suggests that the present time is no more strongly influenced by the past than by the unfolding future. *Kairos* has eschatological overtones; that is, it is associated with the end times, the culmination of history in a moment of judgment and salvation. Yet in Jesus' life, the full power of God for salvation is embodied in present history: all the days of his life are days of the pouring forth of salvation. Jesus lives a life that is drawn and shaped by God's fulfilling and completing purpose; in him, eternity breaks through into the present in a way that makes all things new.

Similarly, we are invited today to live in Jesus in such a way that God's power breaks through into our lives, transforming them and bestowing the abundance for which we long. When we become open to *kairos,* all aspects of our lives are new. Our lives may be broken and limited by past events, but they are healed and made whole by the future poured out through Christ into this now.

For example, today I may really want to have a creative disagreement with my spouse, but I also know that I fear any kind of conflict because my grandmother was unable to control her anger. So, because of my past, I have great difficulty in honestly expressing my own wishes if I think they will irritate another person. But what might happen if I also knew that I could speak the truth in love because the risen Christ is reaching out from the future with a healing touch into my relationship with my spouse today? I will probably feel nervous and awkward, and possibly at first I may slip into a little name-calling or self-blame. But when I trust in Christ's transforming power available to me now, I just may discover that my spouse and I can disagree and actually be relieved to have spoken with each other about this important psychological irritant that has been sitting mutely between us!

At first such an idea seems startling. We psychologically-adept moderns readily understand the present influence of childhood experiences, even if they are long repressed. But can we even imagine the influence of a unique vocation, of God's particular call to each of us, which is transmitted from the end of time into this moment? *Kairos* means that the personal wholeness we have not yet achieved powerfully influences the present moment, because the Word of God is continuously flowing back from the opaque future into the present. We can learn to live in such a way that each ordinary "step in the process of time is a *kairos* in the sense that it is a critical time, a decisive moment which hastens or retards the *kairos* of salvation and judgment."[2]

But what does *kairos* have to do with Benedictine prayer? Benedictine prayer is so profoundly shaped by its attunement to the *kairos* of God in Christ that one cannot be considered apart from the other. The purpose of the Benedictine hours of prayer is to draw its participants daily more and more into the life of Christ, and therefore more and more into the transforming unity of time known in Christ. Praying in the Benedictine way, we are being transformed into Christ's life in every moment, because Christ's presence in time is both expressed in one historical moment and reexperienced in the assembly now praying. Time itself becomes for us a vessel dispensing God's power through Christ's time-transcending life. And we become Christ as praying community in the so-called liturgical hours, or the Divine Office. The purpose of the Benedictine office is to help us become members of Christ's Body in such a way that for us time itself is made holy.

The gathering of the monastic community at the Divine Office has "the special character of moments in the history of salvation (*kairoi*), moments when God permits us to encounter him."[3] It is an essential means of becoming attuned to God's life as it is expressed in time. Prayerful unity with the transformative power of God is not something we can attain by ourselves; it is learned and manifested in communal prayer, in common worship. Benedictine spirituality is centered in this truth and derives its particular character from its commitment to the practice of common prayer as a privileged and time-transcending encounter through Christ with the living God in the power of the Spirit, an encounter which brings transformation into the present historical situations of our lives.

We do not become Christ one by one, each of us tested against an external and private standard of holiness. Rather, we are drawn near God in a privileged way, as a gathering of the faithful, joined to Christ in baptism and members of each other, an organism, a living Body which is Christ bringing us "all together to life everlasting" (RB 72:12).

The Benedictine emphasis on communal prayer and life together is not always comfortable for us. The contemporary resurgence of interest in spirituality usually describes a solitary journey, in part because we are often discouraged when seeking earnest spiritual nurture in our normal worshiping communities. We cannot quite imagine an approach emphasizing the communal that will not minimize individual gifts. Yet the tradition of corporate Christian liturgy embraces powerful spiritual wisdom we individuals have seldom been taught. Exploring the Benedictine roots of the communal office, we will uncover for our personal journeys rich resources that can only be found in corporate worship.

The Rule intends individual fulfillment as an essential aspect of corporate wholeness. Benedict does not forbid individual prayer; on the contrary, he presumes that the prayer of the office will be supplemented with private prayer, as the previous chapters on silence and *lectio divina* certainly make clear. Prayer is to be personal as well as communal. In common prayer, the community offers the corporate gift of the psalms in such a way that each individual's mind learns harmony from the voice (RB 19:7). In private prayer, the individual allows Scripture and tradition to become deeply personal so that common worship is enhanced, as for example when the recitation of the Lord's Prayer becomes a covenant each makes to all (RB 13:13).

With this overall framework in mind, let us turn then to the texts and sources of Benedict's Rule to explore the means he used to facilitate the development of a community prayer attuned to God's *kairos*.

Community Prayer as the Measure of Time

Benedict structured the day around the Divine Office, which he also called the *Opus Dei,* or the Work of God. The term "office," referring to the hours of common prayer, is derived from the notion that prayer is our work, our duty, our service. With the office, Benedict established various focal points throughout the day when the community gathers to call to mind the specific work of God in Christ on our behalf and the transforming presence of God in our midst. We all forget. We forget that we are God's. We forget that time and space are God's. We forget that God is near. We forget that in

Christ love and wholeness are always seeking to break through into our situation. The brief but regular offices throughout the day are ways of training our memory, forming our hearts, and teaching ourselves who we really are. The hours of prayer are ways of being united with Christ, becoming members of his body, consecrated as a spiritual temple. Gathered as a prayerful community in the Divine Office, we are not separated from Christ; as head of the Church, our Lord Christ is himself praying in and through and for us to the Father.

Benedict summarizes the purpose of the Divine Office thus:

> We believe that the Divine Presence is everywhere and that the eyes of the Lord behold the good and evil in every place. Especially do we believe this, without any doubt, when we are assisting at the Divine Office. (RB 19:1-2)

The office is not only a reminder of the divine presence, but also a means of expressing the divine life, with all that this implies about the fullness of time (*kairos*) and God's purpose drawing near and seeking entry into our hearts. In these prayers, we are following Christ: not only learning to be his disciples, but also sharing his own experiences of God, his inner spiritual journey as well as the externals of his life.[4]

The hours of the office punctuate the day, corresponding both to natural rhythms as well as to events in the life of the historical Christ. Benedict's integration of a pattern of communal prayer blends practices in such a felicitous way that his model has formed the basic approach to daily corporate prayer for centuries of Christians.[5]

While all the activities of life are integrated with prayer, the times of communal prayer take priority over everything else. Chapter 43 of the Rule begins with these words:

> At the hour of the Divine Office, as soon as the signal is heard, each one is to lay aside whatever he may be engaged in and hasten to [prayer] with all speed, yet with seriousness, so that no occasion be given for levity. Indeed, let nothing be preferred to the Work of God. (RB 43:1-3)

Here, the Work of God—the Divine Office—is to be preferred above all; in another place, the love of Christ is to be preferred above all (RB 4:21; 72:11). If we assume that Benedict made this parallel construction on purpose, he must have considered the office to embody Christ in some way. These times of daily prayer give us a direct way of loving Christ and putting him first, above everything else, as well as of becoming his body. The daily office expresses this mystery: in it, we pray to Christ and we are Christ praying. As Saint Augustine of Hippo wrote:

> When the body of the Son prays it does not separate its head from itself, but it is the one savior of his body, our Lord Jesus Christ who himself prays for us, and prays in us, and is the object of our prayer....Let us recognize therefore our voices in him and his voice in us.[6]

Thus the Divine Office of Benedict has special power to help us become Christ, and to live into the power of transformation promised in Christ.

Because the daily office is evolved from Jewish prayer forms, it has been part of Christian life from the earliest days of Jesus and his disciples.[7] Benedict built on the tradition of the Jewish prayer times at the two cardinal points, or hinges, of the day: sunrise and sunset. Dawn and dusk were especially significant in a world without electricity, and the metaphors of darkness and light were readily adapted by Christians, extending the gifts of the sun to those of the Son. At dayspring, light overcomes the darkness once again, and we remember that Christ is risen. At vespers, the candles are lit, proclaiming the sheltering presence of God in Christ throughout the darkness to come. The regular rhythm of prayer at these naturally recurring moments involves preparation (in the evening) and celebration (in the morning) which affirms that *kairos* (the fullness of time) is always breaking through into *chronos* (the linear pattern of nature).

All the elaborations of the office into daily, weekly, and annual units are variations on the cycle of waking in readiness and resting in thanksgiving. This rhythmic pattern finds expression both in the outer world and in our inner lives. Our very bodies have natural cycles of activity and rest, intake and elimination. These cycles are essential for long-term health. In nature, day follows night; summer follows winter; fruitfulness follows fallowness. Sometimes we think we can ignore these natural cycles, because we believe we have "conquered nature." But with time, stress or illness generally takes its toll on those who refuse regular rest. A major gift of Benedictine common prayer in our own day is encouraging us to establish a pattern of health-giving physical and spiritual rhythms in our lives, even if one's community of prayer is composed of persons in other places or times.

The Divine Office

Benedict structured the entire day around the hours of the office. Eight times during a twenty-four-hour period his community gathered to offer God praise. The basic pattern of the office is this.

Vigils: before dawn

Lauds: at daybreak

Prime: about 6 A.M., the first hour of the Roman day

Terce: about 9 A.M., the third hour

Sext: about noon, the sixth hour

None: about 3 P.M., the ninth hour

Vespers: at dusk, the end of the work day

Compline: before bed, about 8 P.M.

These times express the natural rhythm of the agrarian day, with heavy work in cool periods and rest in hot periods, and prayer at dawn, dusk, before bed, and at regular intervals which anticipate the next portion of the day's activity. The times of the office are also in tune with the natural rhythms of the human body, giving time for eating and digestion, rest and work.

In his Rule, Benedict gives us a wonderful pattern for our own days, marvelously balancing his desire for a rhythm of prayer to frame all the day's activities with a concern for care of the body and the requirements of routine work. The midday offices (Terce, Sext, and None) are known as the "little hours" because they are very brief. The community gathers for a short time only, to recall together the presence of God and to unite in praise. There is simply an opening verse, a hymn, three psalms, a short reading and response, and the dismissal (RB 17:5). The little hours are not meant to interfere with or substitute for manual or intellectual work, but to remind those about to work of its context.

Each one of the hourly devotions has its own special emphasis drawn from the events and inner experience of Jesus' life. In a sense, the Divine Office is like a work of art: it is reexperienced and reinterpreted every time the community prays. The prayer hours are symbols, pointing toward Someone who cannot be fully contained either in time or in words. Benedict tends not to discuss the underlying symbols or meaning of the hours he establishes, so we look in vain in his Rule for his rationale. Many of his sources, however, did set out interpretations for the hours, as have many of his successors, and we can gather some common and repeated themes.[8]

What follows is an interpretation of the hours drawn from early Christian sources and translated into a contemporary mode. We will look at each office in turn and then ask questions of our own lives. In what way are we praying with Christ? In what way are we learning how Christ himself experienced communion with the living God? In what special way are we seeking to become Christ's body? We will look not only at each single office, but also at the pattern which develops in the daily, weekly, and annual cycles. It is almost as if we are taking our hands and gently tracing the contours of the body of our Lord, letting our sense of touch teach us how we are to be guided as we come to prayer.

No doubt few of us will actually try to pray the daily, weekly, and annual rhythm of the office exactly as Benedict set them out. Indeed, many modern monastic and other worshiping communities have redistributed their prayer to fit their own patterns. But even when we pray alone or pray only a portion of the office, it is good to have a sense of the overall pattern to which we join ourselves in this prayer.

Daily pattern

Benedict's schedule involved a first office of readings, called *Vigils, Matins,* or *Nocturns.* This office is usually prayed in the darkness, roughly around 2 A.M. As the word "vigil" implies, the emphasis of this first office of the day is on keeping watch. It suggests an alertness and an expectancy that God is flowing forth into human life, and an eagerness and preparation for noticing when and how this is happening.

Lauds, the next office, occurs at daybreak, with the appearance of the morning star, or dayspring, and takes its name from the psalms of praise—Psalms 148 to 150—which are normally offered at this time. The appearance of the morning star fulfills a promise. We have not been abandoned and our vigil has been made fruitful in the ever-new appearance of God. This office expresses all the gladness and celebration that greets the return of the sun (Son) and the assurance of life which corresponds to it. As we might imagine, its theme is praise, again suggested by the word itself, for in Latin, *laudate* is a command to praise.

Prime, which shortly follows Lauds in Benedict's scheme, is intended to express a response to praise and adoration of God. It is oriented toward dedication and preparation for the day's labors, in the sure knowledge of God's aid and good will. The name of this office comes from its occurrence at the first hour of the day, and a reliance on God's help which is necessary at the beginning of anything (RB Prologue:4).[9]

The next three hours are brief offices recited during the mid-section of the day and are associated in early Christian usage with specific moments recorded in the New Testament, especially those of Christ's passion and resurrection. *Terce* (about 9 A.M.) asks for strength, particularly that inner strengthening which comes from the Holy Spirit (Acts 2:1-15). *Sext* (about noon) marks a moment full of conflict. Jesus is nailed to the cross and darkness covers the land (Matt. 27:45). Our passions are at their height. Crisis signifies both danger and opportunity; if temptation is great, so is the opportunity to renew one's self-offering to God. In recent years the daily Eucharist is often offered at this hour, immediately following Sext. Finally, *None* expresses perseverence. Christ endured to complete his mission and we are invited to choose to hold fast to him in the heat of the day as we grow tired. Jesus' cry from the cross, from Psalm 22, expresses despair, but embodies assurance as well, for "dominion belongs to the Lord" (Ps. 22:28).

Vespers marks the service of lamplighting, corresponding to the rising of the evening star. At this time of the day, labor is over and there is thanksgiving for the presence and care of God throughout the day. The scriptural theme at this hour is the completion and bringing to fulfillment of the passion of our Lord. Sometimes this is focused on the Last Supper (especially the narrative prayer in John 17), and sometimes on the death of Christ, the completion of his human work that would show God's action in the great new resurrection of the morning.

Just as the great morning office of Lauds is followed by a short office (Prime) embodying personal response to the work of God in this moment, so the great evening office of Vespers is followed by *Compline*. Compline and Prime are both oriented toward dedication and reliance on God, trust and confidence in his care. If Vespers symbolizes the fulfillment of Christ's work in death, then Compline helps us submit gladly to the mini-death of night and sleep, confessing both our needs and God's protection.

So the inner pattern of the prayer is this: we begin by being radically *attentive* to and expectant of God's coming, we *praise* God for the gift of life, then *dedicate* ourselves to God in preparation for the day. During the day we seek that *strength* beyond ourselves which alone enables us to live fully (RB Prologue:41), acknowledging that we often experience *conflict* and darkness, and simply *persevere* in faith when we can do no more. At evening time we give *thanks* for the day and its *fullness,* and rededicate ourselves to *reliance* on God, acknowledging our need for divine care. And we find the cycle completed only in its renewal: *expectant,* we discover that God has come, and we give *thanks.* This is not usually the pattern we envision when we think about abundant life! It sounds full of struggle and difficulty, and never attains that personal triumph we tend to associate with success and satisfaction.

We might ask, what is the point of all this? Aren't all these details a bit much, and don't they remove spontaneity and personal encounter from prayer? Doesn't this rhythm get old fairly quickly, dissolving merely into a rote recitation of set prayers? Most especially, we might ask whether this really has anything to do with our initial desire that God be sensibly present, making a difference for us in ordinary life. Do these hours and symbols really have anything to do with us twentieth-century people?

Let's consider what this pattern might look like in an ordinary life. Someone who prays these hours every day for a month is building habits of mind and heart that will shape the flow of each day. She has expectancy and attentiveness, looking for something special in the day. She notices the wonder and beauty of the world, and offers herself to cooperate with it. She seeks strength outside herself for this cooperation. She recognizes the temptation to forget goodness and beauty, and she recommits herself not to collude with the forces of cynicism and despair all around her. She perseveres, placing her whole trust in God, even when something in herself seems to be dying, and gradually she finds she is giving thanks for the experience of wonder and beauty in and around her.

If we apply this pattern to a particular life issue, how would it work? Let us imagine a woman who has just recovered memories of childhood abuse. This woman is feeling hopeless, perhaps suicidal, conscious of self-hatred so deep that it may seem to her better that she were dead. Wisely, she is receiving therapy, both in individual and group settings, and gradually she comes to believe that there may be a way to heal the terrible pain which she has covered up and disguised for so many years. At the same time, she turns to the prayer of the Church, the Divine Office, hoping that it will aid the inner healing process. She prays Matins, experiencing to the full the dangers and fears of the darkness of night, and sees the break of day with hungry eyes, realizing in the ancient prayers a kindred voice raised in awe at the hope revealed in the eternal promise of the new day arriving.

Continuing in the pattern of the office, she may acknowledge that she feels dread at the tasks the day will require, but she is also willing to let the Spirit pray through her and to welcome the possibility, at least, that some beauty and wonder may be given to her this day. She consents to be receptive, and when a friend calls at midday to tell her how much she appreciated her honesty in last night's conversation, and how it helped her face the next day, our woman allows herself a moment of delight and warmth in this welcome human touch. And when, an hour later, she experiences a panic attack, she reminds herself of the earlier call, and receives strength from knowing she is not alone.

Day by day she perseveres, willing to experience the suffering and self-doubt that inevitably come with a true cleansing of an old wound, in the faith that there is Someone strong, willing her good, actively drawing her through grief into a future wholeness. When she forgets and doubts, she simply continues with the prayer of the daily office, grateful for the unity she feels with people long ago and still to come who are in some way suffering with her. Gradually the center of balance in her life changes, and she discovers a delight in the world and herself she had never imagined possible. What the tradition has done in punctuating her day with the remembrance of Christ is to provide her with a remarkably apt map of the psychological terrain she must negotiate everyday.

In the most serious and most trivial events of life, we find in the office, in the pattern of Christ's life and passion, strength for our journeys. The hours of the office address the ebb and flow of attention and intention that daily move through our spirits, no matter who we are. The gift of Christ's incarnation and earthly existence has long been known to correspond to the need of human lives for daily direction. The office provides a way to grow increasingly receptive to the Risen Christ who seeks to be part of our ordinary lives. In it, we are following the historical Christ through key outer and inner moments which teach us a great deal about the content of our own lives and about how to become God's new creation.

Weekly pattern

The weekly pattern of the Work of God is very similar to the sacramental themes of the daily pattern. Sunday is the day of resurrection, corresponding to Lauds. The Son arises, and God is manifest in fullness—creating, redeeming, and sanctifying. Monday is like Prime, taking in the truth that God is with us, and dedicating ourselves to the divine life and purpose. Tuesday is like Terce, expressing awareness that our actions are important and seeking the strengthening of the Holy Spirit in the continuing choice for life. Wednesday, like None, is the midpoint crisis of danger and opportunity, accentuated by the recollection of Judas' betrayal. Thursday takes on some of the characteristics of Vespers, and is traditionally associated with the fulfillment and anticipation of the Lord's Supper. Friday emphasizes the other half of Vespers' meaning, associated with the passion and death of the Lord, the completeness of surrender into God's hands. Saturday blends Compline and Matins, in its dark blindness and expectant confidence in God who is not yet seen, but who has promised to reveal all things in the fullness of time. And Sunday concludes as well as begins the cycle, with the triumphant and joyous victory of God, bringing new life and resurrection into the world against all odds.

Again, we observe the patterns of mind and heart taught in the weekly practice of the office. We start by celebrating that the world is fully God's. We continue by dedicating and preparing ourselves to cooperate with God in history, and acknowledging that our actions contribute to or diminish God's work. We admit the limits of our own capacity even as we offer ourselves to God. Wonderfully, we find that our need for help is more than met by God's life given freely to us. As we surrender more and more to God, we find ourselves in a darkness of faith that is expectant. This pattern of spiritual formation can be discovered and rediscovered in the context of every life with the help of the office as reminder and guide.

Again, a specific example may help us to understand better what daily prayer throughout the week accomplishes in us. This time, let us visualize a man who has been taken over by a nagging inner restlessness, despite the fact that everything in his life is going very well. He is affirmed and appreciated in a job he likes. He and his wife have a good relationship, and he enjoys his two growing children. He is an active member of a local parish, and this year he is chairman of a major committee there. And yet something is missing. There is a haunting interior emptiness that seems strangely at variance with the exterior facts. He takes his perplexity to the parish priest, who suggests that he begin attending the daily Vespers service in the chapel. At first, he is a little disappointed by the advice, thinking that the priest didn't take him very seriously. But after a week or two, he is surprised to discover that each afternoon he eagerly looks forward to the office. For some reason it has become a high point in his day.

Sunday he goes to church, and he cannot stop the tears when he comes forward for the Eucharist—that God should care so much for him! And he tells himself, "The world is God's, and I am, too." Monday, his prayer is that he be willing to seek God's will in all things. Tuesday evening he prays the office with special intensity, aware that Wednesday he has an interview with an influential corporation whose account he is trying to swing to his agency. He does his best in the interview, and Wednesday evening he is strangely peaceful at Vespers. When he finds out on Thursday that he didn't get the account, he is disappointed but not devastated, feeling he presented his company well and fairly and somehow, sometime, his work will bear fruit. He says to himself, "What I do matters, at least to God! And I know God will give me and my company what we most need, if we are faithful to him."

By Friday evening, he finds that he is more distressed than on Thursday because his business associates don't have the peace he feels and they think of him as a loser. But he doesn't skip the office on either Friday or Saturday, and he manages to find a little more time than usual to spend with his kids. Saturday evening when the children are out with friends, he and his wife rent a movie and make popcorn and hold hands on the sofa, and he is filled with a strange contentment.

On Sunday, a phrase from one of the psalms plants itself in his mind so that he carries it to work on Monday and throughout the following week: "Uphold me, Lord, according to your word, and I shall live" (Ps. 119:116; RB 58:21). He realizes that before, he was existing but not living. The outer standards of success or failure didn't really touch his heart. It was *life* he missed and was restless without. Week after week he continues with the office, and gradually he finds something changing inside him. Life no longer feels so flat, but now seems full of delight and gratitude. And the restlessness is gone!

Annual pattern

Christian liturgy proclaims the good news about new life. Each Sunday is a remembrance of Easter Sunday, when God acted decisively in history to reveal the divine intention and power to bring abundant new life out of even the worst situation. As every Sunday is a reminder of Easter, so every morning is a reminder of Sunday: through the office, we remember that the resurrection is always bursting forth in our midst, inviting our consent and cooperation. The daily pattern corresponds to the weekly, the weekly to the annual. The effective promise of transformation, of *kairos* breaking into human life as definitively as at Easter, is the center of the daily office.

The annual pattern for the Benedictine office is centered around the Easter celebration. Benedict described two major seasons, between Easter and fall ("summer season") and between fall and Easter ("winter season").[10] These seasonal shifts are not just "spiritual"; they are also reflected in the number of meals (RB 41) and the schedule of work (RB 48). The Easter feast governs working and eating as well as praying. In the Rule, there is one unified celebration of our world's primary relation to its Creator. Easter is the capstone of the year, and Sunday is the weekly celebration and remembrance of Easter. Every sunrise expresses this miracle.

The annual calendar actually contains two parallel cycles, one major and one minor. Each cycle consists of a period of preparation, a time of celebration, and a period of integration of the celebrated mystery.[11] Easter is the major cycle, with the Lenten preparation and Pentecost the period of integration. The minor cycle of Christmas anticipates and points toward Easter. Here Advent is the period of preparation and Epiphany the period of integration. Each cycle has designated readings from Scripture for the office, which bring particular sacred events into remembrance in the life of the people of God.

For example, Benedict's chapter on the observance of Lent makes it clear that the purpose of Lent is personal preparation, "awaiting Easter with the joy of spiritual longing" (RB 49:7). In this season, both the readings from Scripture and the psalms in the office with their antiphons are oriented toward preparation. The gathered community recalls the evidences of God's will and God's promises to the people throughout the long period of God's fidelity to them. There is also reading and reflection on the ways in which God's people have fallen short and hardened their hearts to the promises. The whole focus is on being expectant and ready for the powerful work that God has done, is doing, and will do on Easter, the day of resurrection.

We see how similar this annual pattern is to the daily and weekly patterns of living into Christ's outer and inner life. We observed that the inner pattern of the daily office begins with radical *attention* and the expectation that God will come; we *praise* God for the gift of life that is given. This is of course very similar to Advent and Christmas. Then in the daily rhythm, we *dedicate* ourselves to God in preparation for the day. In the annual cycle, Epiphany involves the integration of the gift of God's own life given in Christmas, with an increasing realization of how that life burns brightly in each of us. We dedicate ourselves to God in preparation for the year to come.

At midday, we seek beyond ourselves that *strength* which alone enables us to live fully (RB Prologue:41), acknowledging that we often experience *conflict* and darkness, and simply *persevere* in faith when we can do no more. Similarly, in Lent we pray for strength to repent and cleanse ourselves so that we may grow in freedom to choose God; during Passion Week, we experience conflict and darkness to the full, and we endure.

At evening, we give *thanks* for the day and its *fullness,* and rededicate ourselves to *reliance* on God, acknowledging our need for divine care. And we find the cycle completed only in its renewal: *expectant,* we discover that God has come, and we give *thanks.* And so at last in the annual pattern, Easter comes and then Pentecost, with its gift of the Spirit's life to our own. And we begin this life-bringing, cyclical inner rhythm again.

As a contemporary example of someone praying the annual cycle of the office, we might consider the life of a nineteen-year-old boy who is mentally retarded and has ongoing deterioration from muscular dystrophy.[12] The young man and his parents might (and sometimes do) rage at God for the unfairness of these afflictions, or they might worry over what sin or psychic debility is expressing itself in his life. But as they pray through the church year, they find themselves first in the somber period of Advent, joining the faithful in serious consideration of the truth that the future is God's, and though it is filled with tension and distress, there is still cause for celebration because God is with us. No distress can overtake us that does not also carry the full power of God's life in its midst. With his simplicity, the young man hears this word and takes it to heart. At Christmas, he is unself-consciously happy to celebrate the reality of his daily experience and the fullness of his hope: "Jesus is with me." In Epiphany his love shines like a beacon to many who turn away in discomfort from his obvious suffering.

In Lent, his parents begin to take lessons from Christ in their son; they begin letting go of attitudes and possessions which separate them from God's nearness. Though their grief is not diminished, a feeling of peace seems to grow in its midst so that they can fully participate with Christ in the sufferings of Passion Week, and are astonished to be filled with joy at the extraordinary beauty and radiance emanating from their son on Easter Day. And in Pentecost they sense so fully the abiding presence of God's Holy Spirit that they are able to bury their son in the late fall with courage and hope. When, in the spring, they find themselves missing his delight in the first new blossoms on the trees, they have begun to know in their hearts that now their son is continuously rapt in the joy he so often expressed while in this life.

The annual pattern of the Divine Office is full of the reality of life and death, and traces two parallel themes, one from the Hebrew Scriptures and one from the New Testament. The Hebrew theme centers on the Exodus of the children of Israel from Egypt. God created them and chose them for special intimacy. When they were enslaved in Egypt, God miraculously freed them and brought them forth. But they were not ready for freedom, and wandered in the desert for forty years being taught maturity. Finally, they were brought into the Promised Land, the land of abundance and prosperity. But they fared no better there, allowing prosperity to enslave them as surely as poverty had in Egypt. So the cycle began again.

Each time the people remember their story, they take heart and begin again in hope. Each time they experience some form of failure, and are yet restored by the mercy of God. So it is today: we people of God keep on remembering, that we may see where and how this cycle is manifest in our own lives. We remember, looking at how we have been chosen. We remember, observing that we often make choices that seem like slavery. We remember, noticing that God restores us each time we return. We too take heart and begin anew to hope to be received in mercy.

The New Testament takes up these same themes of creation, covenant, refusal, enslavement, and redemption. But there one person takes up this whole enactment on behalf of all the people—God does for us what we are powerless to do for ourselves. God fully present in Jesus Christ becomes fully human as we are. Through fidelity to his unique life, Jesus intervenes in the pattern of enslavement and isolation of God's people. Jesus, giving himself fully to us humans, restores the natural connection between the creation and the Creator so that it can never be broken again. He brings into existence the power of renewal and transformation so that it is always and fully present in every corner of the created world. Yet we are given to understand that the final fulfillment of this story is only made complete as we pray and live into our own part of the story here and now.

This annual pattern of readings and prayers is intended to help situate each of our journeys toward God in the context of the journey of God's people through time. It helps bring God's presence—past and future—into our own time. It brings God's life into our own life, and our life into God's. In the readings, we hear over and over again the patterns of creation, brokenness, and transformation enacted in the life of the body of the Church, of which we are a living part. Through the annual, daily, and weekly offices we find in Christ's life a model of being in relation to God that helps us re-pattern our own lives. And these patterns of the office are increasingly seen to be the patterns of our own lives, the stuff of our own struggles, the reason for our hope.

Why do these themes of the Old and New Testaments keep emphasizing brokenness as well as wholeness, isolation as well as communion, enslavement as well as freedom, sin as well as redemption? If God is good and powerful and always working for transformation, and if in Christ's resurrection God's power is definitively victorious, why then do the events of Jesus' passion and death loom so large in our daily, weekly, and annual celebrations? Why must we keep remembering these old cycles of fall and rescue? Our lives are bad enough. Why must we keep praying all these negative images, all these reminders of failure and brokenness and death?

If this is transformation, we might well ask, who wants it? In our examples, we have a woman who must live through the pain of terrible memories, a man who does not get an important business account, a boy who dies. Is this transformation? In our biblical examples, we find a Hebrew people scattered and in exile and a holy man whose reward was to be killed on a cross. To give ourselves to Christian transformation, we need to see clearly this paradox, this irony, this challenge. And we need to learn to see how and where it is manifest in our own lives, and to cooperate with it.

Benedict's office teaches and reveals one important truth: death *precedes* life. Good Friday is the doorway into Easter Sunday. We may have thought we were alive, but we have not yet been born. In the Divine Office, we share Christ's death in order that we may rise with him in the resurrection of new life. The prayer of the office teaches and empowers us to die into life.

In the beginning we pray because we want something from God, because we need something in our lives that we cannot provide for ourselves. If we want to have abundant life, then we must give ourselves over to the pattern of spiritual life we learn in the liturgical year. Transformation *is* promised, but not on our terms and not in our way. True transformation follows God's ways, which are built into the structure of creation and modeled for us in the life of Christ. True transformation leads from death into life. We cannot willingly die by ourselves, so we seek in our cycle of prayers to become like Jesus Christ and to receive his life in order to follow him through the narrow door of death that leads to abundant life (RB Prologue:48).

The daily office helps us to remember and to hope. To remember is not to talk nostalgically about how good things used to be. To hope is not to proclaim vigorously how good things will be. To remember and to hope is to become part of the story, to die as we must and to awake to the new life eager to be born within ourselves and our situations. This is the work of Benedict's hours of prayer through the day, week, and year. This is Benedict's way of community prayer, open to the fullness of God's time for transformation in human life.

Transformation in Daily Life

Let us explore the implications of this transformative prayer for our own lives. We may have a vague understanding of what it means to lose life in order to find it, but it almost always comes as a shock to realize that at certain moments we are confronted with a specific opportunity for death. Such opportunities may be as straightforward (and excruciating) as giving up a compulsion to alcohol, work, or overprotectiveness. They may be as painful as accepting the actual loss of a spouse, limb, cherished possession, or valued employment. They may be as subtle and complex as the willingness to risk an unknown opportunity, first giving up a known and comfortable place. However well we understand the process in general, when we accept the specific invitation posed to us by our life experience, the loss always *feels* like a death.

Benedict's Rule is particularly helpful in this regard, because Benedict so often recognizes the trials of life in community as opportunities for the little deaths which help us become the Christ in whom we pray. For example, the business manager is to respond to an unreasonable request not with a sharp retort, but with a kind word (RB 31:7, 13-14). The abbot is not to bolster his authority by dissension and quarrels (RB 65:7-9). The porter is to greet continual interruption by guests by receiving each one as Christ himself (RB 66:3-4; 53:6-7). Members are always to consider what is better for another (RB 72:7). All are to be content with the most common and worst of everything (RB 7:49). At first glance, these instructions seem either very easy—just become a doormat—or very hard. We have no idea how to let such truth and power in love spring forth from the deepest level of our being; we do not have the resources or the inner freedom, humanly speaking.

The paschal pattern of the Divine Office demands to be taken seriously in our ordinary life; we are sent from the office directly into the opportunities for dying embodied in our daily life. Many Christians would generously die heroically for Christ—but little daily deaths are harder to accept. If only they did not *feel* like dying; if only there were certainty of new life afterwards! Our culture supports us in avoiding death and suffering; indeed, much popular spirituality suggests that the truly "spiritual" person does not need to suffer, does not need to experience loss, does not need to give anything up.

But Benedict's understanding of the gospel, as expressed in the prayer of the office, is that the only way to abundant life is to go *through* death; we are not free to ignore or distract ourselves from suffering, if we would truly be transformed. We must follow the pattern toward new life modeled by our Lord: if we would gain our life, then we must lose it. We must keep death daily before our eyes (RB 4:47).

We often experience the painful situations of our lives as very much worse than they are because we actively resist them. It is possible through the prayer of the office to discover that our life situations are more bearable when we become able to accept them and submit to them, through Christ and in the power of God's Spirit. Jesus Christ is our example, as he bears his suffering with patience, not passively but actively embracing the pain because he knows God's love is in its midst, somewhere beyond his understanding (RB 7:35).

These are hard sayings, but gradually we can learn to recognize them as being the only thing that makes sense out of otherwise senseless suffering. Only the Judeo-Christian faith dares to take seriously both the transcendent glory of life in God and the often perplexing pain of being fully present to the human struggles which are part of every life. The paschal model tells us that all these little deaths—sundered relationships, lost employment, surgical and natural physical losses, lowered pride and self-esteem—all these deaths mean something. All these deaths are preparing us for something so glorious we cannot imagine it. All these deaths lead in the divine economy to radiant new life. Dying, we have hope.

A middle-aged religious sister commits her life to helping the urban poor. She devotes herself day and night to the families in a slum neighborhood, often wearied beyond measure at the institutions that perpetuate conditions of the most appalling harshness, and her prayer is frequently a helpless cry to God for justice. She knows that Benedictine prayer does not condone injustice and is not a handy substitute for fighting exploitation. In the course of her ministry, she has often been called to live into the kind of death that involves abandoning her "good reputation" in order to stand on the side of the victim. Yet recently she has been troubled by an inner fantasy of walking up to the door of the biggest local slumlord and bashing him in the face! She accepts this anger as a natural feeling, and even a healthy one, but she is distressed at the recurring and specific projection of hostility against a single human being as if he were the embodiment of all evil.

One day during the office, her community prays Psalm 137, in which the psalmist cries out for revenge against his enemies, asking that blessing be bestowed on anyone who hurls their babies to a rocky death (verse 9). She smiles to herself, glad for a moment that her ancestors in faith also had hostile fantasies, but then remembers how Benedict prayed this psalm as a way of laying open his own temptations to Christ (RB Prologue:28; 4:50). Right then, she offers up her fantasy to God. In the peace that follows, she suddenly realizes how angry she is at God for allowing so much suffering of the innocent. In her many years of service, this woman has not even made a dent in the horror of life in her neighborhood, and she is both resentful and righteously outraged that anyone dare call himself good while allowing such injustice.

She realizes that there is yet another death she must die, and that involves giving up the desire to make a difference. She also feels herself called to give up the relative comfort of her self-image as one who does good, to acknowledge in herself the same impulses toward aggression (such as her desire to smash the landlord's power) that she has judged so severely in others. How much she hates to admit the dishonesty and distortions in her own thoughts and motives; how much easier it would be to go on thinking of herself as a righteous crusader for good. Can she bear to go on carrying out her day-to-day tasks, knowing how false her motives often are? Will she lose effectiveness if she loses her passionate hatred for the oppressive forces in society? Can she live humbly among these poor, willing simply to give and receive love among them, without knowing if or whether she is making any difference in the grand scheme of things? She cannot escape herself, and she doesn't know how to change. This is truly the invitation to death, and she is free to choose among many options. What will she choose?

We *can* choose death, but life is always a gift. And yet the clear message of the office is that crucifixion is never the last chapter; death always precedes life, not the other way around. Apparently there is some hidden secret in the willingness to give oneself without reservation to "impossible" things that provides an opening for the power of God to work good in the midst of an unlikely place (see RB 68). The crux of Benedictine communal prayer is the daily offering of our lives and all they contain to God for God's own care and guidance, for that is the way to life. The free offering to God of all that we are, including our helplessness, is the gift we make to God. And before we have completed our gesture of offering, God rushes to us, calling to us, "Behold, I am here" (Isa. 58:9; RB Prologue:18).

Easter and resurrection are theological terms for the issues with which we began our consideration of Benedictine prayer. We turn to God needing something we cannot name. We seek from God the fulfillment of the promise of new creation in our ordinary moments. We yearn for a transformation of our way of being in the world, a transformation that brings with it the fullness of love, joy, and peace. In the celebration of Easter, we are raised into the very life of God, and we know what it is to be whole. This is the Divine Office: a privileged moment when each and all remember and know who we are, joining the praise of all creation for the wonder of life. Transformation is not just "out there" in the future, but actually "in here," because we are becoming what we behold.

When we speak of radical new life, we use images and metaphors to suggest something which lies within but also beyond the parameters of our experience and inner vision. One fourth-century author speaks of stages, including an actual liturgy, a liturgy of the heart, and finally an exalted and rare stage called the "heavenly liturgy."[13] This heavenly liturgy, or common prayer, is always a gift given by God. To receive this gift is already to participate mysteriously in the heavenly life, even as we remain on earth and do not cease celebrating the visible liturgy and the liturgy of the heart.

The prayer of the office gradually leads us to become aware of elements in daily experience to which we were previously blind. It resembles a whistle, pitched out of range of human hearing but perfectly audible to animals. In this case, we are talking about a quality of human experience, an abundance and transformation that penetrates into daily life. It is out of the range of our senses, but the office gradually shapes our capacity to receive it in a fulfilling way. There is still the element of ambiguity; such experience cannot be given away to anyone else, nor can it be "proved" in a series of experimental tests. Yet the quality of our lives is radically new, exactly as the lives of the eleven disciples changed when the risen Christ came to them. Thomas Keating, searching for words to describe this transformation, says that the celebration of communal prayer "does not offer us a mere seat in the bleachers or even a ringside seat. We are invited to participate in the event itself...[to become] manifestations of the Gospel in the shifting shapes, forms and colors of daily life."[14]

Living the gospel is about being in love. It is knowing that we are never alone. It is knowing ourselves to be loved, and therefore lovable. It is delight that a being exists with whom there is such union of mind, heart, spirit. It is astonishment that such an improbable and wonderful thing could come to be—a glorious communion that is stronger and more beautiful than any amount of pain. It does not necessarily mean that all the external circumstances of our lives change for the better, but that we see them anew in the light of a compassion for all things. We retain passionate loves and strong opinions. We still suffer and die, but the new life beyond death rests in the certainty that all is in God's hands, and that is enough.

Saint Paul reminds us that we hope for things not seen (Rom. 8:24). None of us can sustain this transformed way of living, day in and day out. We all forget; we all lose heart; we all experience the natural alternation of faith and doubt, hope and despair, being lifted up and being cast down. We all continue to die and be reborn. Hope has to do with things intangible, things not yet seen, things only hinted at in our experience. And yet, Paul adds, hope does not disappoint us (Rom. 5:5).

We live in *chronos,* duration; yet in the Divine Office of Saint Benedict *kairos,* possibility, breaks through into our lives. In common prayer, we are transformed. The future unfolds opportunity for us; as the body of Christ in the present we remember the past. The future is unknown and therefore for some of us fearful, unmanageable, and hostile. Yet as we remember God's past presence, we come to a new understanding of the future, and we can hope. We may choose to sit down and immerse ourselves in cool delight, feeling little swirls and eddies lap about our ankles, or we may try to take a big broom and sweep back the ocean. We still have choice, just as we do in choosing the ways our past will influence us. But we cannot interact creatively with either future or past until we are aware of them and their pull upon us.

What image helps us see this possibility, this way of inviting the future into our lives through our prayer? I think of a sketch by Raphael of a naked infant rushing forward and upward in great delight, lifting his arms in absolute confidence. That is the whole picture, except for one adult hand stretching down to the child's waist to help lift him up. This is a picture of how God comes through the future to us—not entirely visible, not entirely invisible, yet always in love and strength.

What is a transformed life like? Benedict himself gives us hints of his answer in his character sketch of the cellarer (RB 31). He used the language of his time, but a slow reflective reading of his description yields a keen sense of what the cellarer must have been like. As the business manager of the monastic community, he is to be like a father to the whole community. He gives the brothers everything they need for life—food, clothing, tools, and equipment. As steward of the community's possessions, he is guardian of many treasures, but he is to use these treasures in a way that ensures the attentive care of all.

The cellarer acts without delay in response to a request, but he never rushes or frets. He could easily be the center of much competitive rivalry, but instead he seems to be a center of peace; people come to him when they need a word of encouragement. So great is his respect for things as well as people that even the kitchen pots are cared for no less lovingly than the altar vessels. The circumstances of his job would seem to create busyness and anxiety, yet here we find a man who radiates a loving and generous openness to life! This is someone who cannot hide the abiding presence of God in his person; he has clearly received resurrection in his own life.[15]

The portrait that emerges is one of power willing to be spent in the subtle and unassuming toil of gentle presence in the daily round. Perhaps the glorious new life on the other side of death often expresses itself very simply in the smallest of moments. Could it be that we know so little about transformation into the life of God because we have been looking for it in the wrong garb?

Endnotes

1. Two good contemporary discussions of these concepts of time are James D. and Evelyn E. Whitehead, *Method in Ministry* (New York: Seabury, 1980), pp. 149-151; and Douglas C. Vest, *Why Stress Keeps Returning* (Chicago: Loyola University Press, 1991), pp. 28-29.

2. John L. McKenzie, *Dictionary of the Bible* (New York: Macmillan and London: Collier Macmillan, 1965), p. 892.

3. "The Hours of the Work of God," No. 9 in *Directory for the Celebration of the Work of God:* Guidelines for the Monastic Liturgy of the Hours Approved for the Benedictine Confederation (Riverdale, Md.: Exordium Books, 1981), p. 25.

4. See Bernadette Roberts, "The Eucharist: A Christian Path," in *Studies in Formative Spirituality,* Volume VIII, No. 3 (November, 1987), especially p. 349. She says: "What [Christ] wished for us was

that we too discover the inner source and from this same source work out our own historical lives, manifest the source in whatever circumstances we might find ourselves."

5. For more detail on the gradual historical developments in the monastic office in general, see such sources as *RB 1980*, Appendix 3, "The Liturgical Code in the Rule of Benedict," especially pp. 379-389. Consult as well: Cheslyn Jones, Geoffrey Wainwright, Edward Yarnold, SJ, eds., *The Study of Liturgy* (New York: Oxford University Press, 1978); and Paul F. Bradshaw, *Daily Prayer in the Early Church: A Study of the Origin and Early Development of the Divine Office* (London: SPCK, Alcuin Club, 1981).

6. Saint Augustine's *Discourse* on Psalm 85:1, as quoted in "General Instructions on the Liturgy of the Hours," part of the Conciliar and Post-Conciliar Documents of Vatican II, Section II.7. The abridged form of the "General Instructions" can be found in *Christian Prayer: The Liturgy of the Hours* (New York: Catholic Book Publishing Co., 1976), pp. 8-19. Augustine's quotation is found in this edition on page 12.

7. For a particularly good, succinct statement of the part of daily prayer in the earliest church, see the "General Instruction on the Liturgy of the Hours," I and II, as well as Bradshaw, *Daily Prayer in the Early Church*. Benedict himself consolidated two main patterns of the office extant in his time, combining elements of the cathedral office and the monastic office. In so doing, he eased the sometimes severe monastic practice. For example, he removed the standard Saturday all-night vigil and stretched out the period in which all the psalms were to be recited to one week instead of one day. But Benedict also expanded the cathedral practice into a pattern providing more firmness for the whole day. See *RB 1980*, Appendix 3: "The Liturgical Code in the Rule of Benedict," and "Ancient Tradition and New Creation," No. 19 in *Directory for the Celebration of the Work of God*.

8. It is clear that as early as the fourth or fifth century there were already specific patterns of daily prayer, designed to recall the saving actions of Christ in the context of daily life. Benedict would have been quite familiar with symbolic interpretations of the office, for they appear in the writings of Augustine, Athanasius, Tertullian, Cyprian, and Cassian, to name a few of his predecessors.

Contemporary discussions of the meaning of the hours of prayer can be found in the books noted earlier in this chapter, as well as in Michael Downey, "Rhythms of the Word," *Cistercian Studies Quarterly* Vol. 26/2 (1991), pp. 152-164; and Charles E. Miller, CM, *Making Holy the Day* (New York: Catholic Book Publishing Co., 1975).

9. In contemporary practice, Prime and Lauds are often combined. The office of Prime, as introduced by Benedict, has been omitted from the Benedictine-Cistercian *horarium* in recent years on the basis of modern liturgical scholarship.

10. There is variation in the beginning of the winter season in the Rule: liturgically, it begins on the "first of November" (RB 8:1), but as regards meals, it begins September 14, and as regards work, it begins on the first of October. See *RB 1980*, pp. 408-409.

11. "The Three Temporal Cycles," Section 11 in *Directory for the Celebration of the Work of God*, p. 27, states this threefoldness as announcement, fulfillment, and prolongation. The point is that past, present, and future are all sacramentally reexperienced in a transforming way as the community prays the Divine Office together.

12. This example is taken from a powerful meditation on suffering and helplessness called simply *Scott*, by Christopher Jones (Springfield, Ill.: Templegate Publishers, 1978).

13. André Louf, OCSO, "The Work of God: A Way of Prayer" in *Cistercian Studies Quarterly*, Vol. 26/1 (1991), p. 66. The fourth-century document from which he quotes is the *Book of Degrees*, a collection of thirty discourses in Syriac.

14. Thomas Keating, OCSO, *The Mystery of Christ: The Liturgy as Spiritual Experience* (New York: Amity House, 1987), p. 8.

15. Compare the story about Benedict himself in Gregory's *Life*, chapter 21, pp. 47f.

Exercises in Prayer

One

In his Rule, Benedict calls for two special psalms to be recited at Lauds on each day of the week (RB 13:4-9). Monday has Psalms 5 and 36, Tuesday Psalms 43 and 57, Wednesday Psalms 64 and 65, Thursday Psalms 88 and 90, Friday Psalms 76 and 92, Saturday Psalm 143 and the Canticle from Deuteronomy (Deut 31:30-32:43). For one week, take some time each day to read these daily psalms, asking yourself the question, "What, if anything, do these words have to do with me today?"

Perhaps one or two friends would agree to do this exercise during the same week, and you could meet afterwards to discuss your experiences.

Two

The basic model for each of the daily offices is:

Begin with a hymn.

Read a psalm (or several psalms).

Read a passage from Scripture.

Pray.

Using this basic model, develop a simple format of your own for a daily prayer time lasting fifteen or twenty minutes, and try it out for a month. If possible, get a friend to share the practice with you.

Three

Consider applying some portion of Benedict's office in your particular life setting. For example, at your lunch-break, you might like to take a few moments for Sext. As we saw, the theme of this office is crisis, meaning danger and opportunity. We are inclined to forget God at this midday hour, to feel far from the nurture of God's light.

For at least one month, use the format of hymn, psalm, reading, and prayer for a noonday office. Depending on your privacy, you might wish to sing a favorite hymn or softly do a simple chant, such as "Lord, show me the path of life." A good noonday psalm is any portion of Psalm 119, 19, 42, or 56. The Scripture passage should be very short, and one you can fruitfully ponder in silence for a few moments. For example:

> You, O Lord, are in the midst of us, and we are called by your name: Do not forsake us! (Jer. 14:9)

> In your steadfast love you led the people whom you redeemed; you guided them by your strength to your holy abode. (Exod. 15:13)

> For if we have been united with him in a death like his, we will certainly be united with him in a resurrection like his. (Rom. 6:5)

Your prayer should include prayers for yourself and others (for the Church, the welfare of the world, and especially for those who suffer) and prayers of thanksgiving.

Four

If you belong to a liturgical church, follow the Sunday lectionary closely throughout the year. (If you don't, urge your pastor to follow the common lectionary for a trial period of time.) As you participate in these times of community worship, ask yourself, what are the connections between the readings this Sunday? Wonder what is being said about the history of God's people by these readings. Explore how these readings touch your life at this moment. Ask what is God saying to you now in these readings. Consider what impact, if any, these lessons might have for your future and the future of the world. Talk with fellow church members about their reflections on these matters.

Five

If you belong to a community which says or sings the office together, for one week concentrate on the following ways in which community is *embodied* in the office:

a) Be aware of the voices on your right and left, front and back. Keep the volume of your own voice such that you can hear clearly the voices of those four others (and they can hear you). Consider that awareness as a metaphor of diversity in unity, and see if you can apply it to your next heated conversation with someone.

b) Pray the psalms antiphonally (alternating sides), dividing them at mid-verse. As you listen to the two sides alternating, be aware that each is saying very much the same thing in different words. Consider this as a metaphor of Christ being expressed among us, each uniquely in the "words" of our own life.

Six

During a quiet time, ponder how *chronos* and *kairos* are evident in your life. First, make a list of chronological events for some period, say the last twelve months. Then, endeavor to list the kairotic elements which appeared during that same period. Probably your kairotic list will be much shorter, but it will indicate events having a more lasting influence. If you cannot seem to distinguish between the two, reflect on how you envision God acting in your life, if at all.

Seven

Take some quiet time to explore death and life, as daily realities in your own life. When you are relaxed and centered, make a list of about six things you feel are dying right now in your life—things that are fading away, receding, leaving you. These may be skills, hobbies, friendships, or interests. They should be things not quite dead, but dying, diminishing.

Now make a list of about six things that you feel are coming to life right now—things that are emerging, drawing near, coming into being. This list may also include a variety of things. Be as specific as you can.

Now reflect quietly on your two lists. Do you sense that there are things you are doing to help or hinder items on either list? Are items on the lists related to each other? For example, is one thing rising because something dying has made room in your life for it? Is God particularly present in something on either list? When you have taken your reflections as far as you can for now, offer them up to God in trust.

Eight

Pay attention to your own rhythms of energy and rest, and develop a personal daily or weekly schedule of prayer and work, rest and relationship that is most beneficial to you, while also congruent with your commitments. Remember that even brief periods of prayer and rest help give balance to the whole schedule, and even small changes have a cumulative impact. Practice the schedule you develop for a month or so, and see what you discover.

Nine

Follow a daily lectionary for one month. Read a psalm, a portion of the Old Testament, an epistle, and a section from the gospels each day, and combine those readings with a time of quiet and prayer. If you can, find someone else to join you.

Daily lectionaries are available from several traditions: the Roman Catholic *Liturgy of the Hours* has the printed readings in the text; the Episcopal *Book of Common Prayer* and the Lutheran *Book of Worship* list the readings and refer you to your own Bible; the Presbyterian *Daily Prayer Supplemental Liturgical Resource #5* and the Methodist *Book of Worship for Church and Home* and *Supplemental Worship Resources* give a form for the office and list the readings. Various other denominations and groups prepare renewable pamphlets listing the readings and suggesting study questions. Most of these denominational resources also provide regular formats for the two hinge offices of Lauds and Vespers, or Morning and Evening Prayer.

Suggestions for Further Reading

Bondi, Roberti C. *To Love as God Loves: Conversations with the Early Church*. Philadelphia: Fortress Press, 1987.

Bradshaw, Paul F. *Daily Prayer in the Early Church: A Study of the Origin and Early Development of the Divine Office*. London: SPCK, Alcuin Club, 1981.

Cassian, John. *Institutes* and *Conferences*. In Volume XI of *Nicene and Post-Nicene Fathers of the Christian Church*. Translated by Edgar C. S. Gibson. Grand Rapids: Eerdmans, 1986.

Chittister, Joan, OSB. *Wisdom Distilled from the Daily: Living the Rule of St. Benedict Today*. San Francisco: Harper & Row, 1990.

Cummings, Charles, OCSO. *Monastic Practices.* Kalamazoo: Cistercian Publications, 1986.

Deiss, Lucien, CSSp. *Springtime of the Liturgy: Liturgical Texts of the First Four Centuries*. Translated by Matthew J. O'Connell. Collegeville, Minn.: The Liturgical Press, 1979.

Directory for the Celebration of the Work of God: Guidelines for the Monastic Liturgy of the Hours Approved for the Benedictine Confederation. Riverdale, Md: Exordium Books, 1981.

Downey, Michael. "Rhythms of the Word." *Cistercian Studies Quarterly* 26/2 (1991): 152-164.

Evagrius Ponticus. *The Praktikos & Chapters on Prayer.* Translated by John Eudes Bamberger, OCSO. Kalamazoo: Cistercian Publications, 1972.

Fry, Timothy, OSB, ed. *RB 1980: The Rule of St. Benedict in Latin and English with Notes*. Collegeville, Minn.: The Liturgical Press, 1981. See especially the appendices.

Gregory the Great. *The Life and Miracles of St. Benedict*. Translated by Odo J. Zimmermann, OSB and Benedict R. Avery, OSB. Collegeville, Minn.: The Liturgical Press, 1949.

Guigo II the Carthusian. *Ladder of Monks*. Translated by Edmund Colledge, OSA and James Walsh, SJ. Kalamazoo: Cistercian Publications, 1981.

Hatchett, Marion. *Sanctifying Life, Time, and Space: An Introduction to Liturgical Study*. New York: Seabury/Crossroad, 1976.

Hausherr, Irénée, SJ. *Penthos: The Doctrine of Compunction in the Christian East*. Translated by Anselm Hufstader, OSB. Kalamazoo: Cistercian Publications, 1982.

Jones, Christopher. *Scott*. Springfield, Ill.: Templegate Publishers, 1978.

Keating, Thomas, OCSO. *The Mystery of Christ: The Liturgy as Spiritual Experience*. New York: Amity House, 1987.

Leclercq, Jean, OSB. "Silence and Word in the Life of Prayer." *Word and Spirit* 6 (1984).

Louf, André, OCSO. Teach Us To Pray: Learning a Little about God. Translated by Hubert Hoskins. Cambridge, Mass.: Cowley Publications, 1991.

Merton, Thomas. *The Wisdom of the Desert: Sayings from the Desert Fathers of the Fourth Century*. New York: New Directions Books, 1960.

Rees, Daniel, et al. *Consider Your Call: A Theology of Monastic Life Today*. London: SPCK and Kalamazoo: Cistercian Publications, 1978.

Vest, Douglas C. *Why Stress Keeps Returning: A Spiritual Response*. Chicago: Loyola University Press, 1991.

Vest, Norvene. *Bible Reading for Spiritual Growth* (San Francisco: Harper Collins, 1993.

✓ _____. *Preferring Christ: A Devotional Commentary and Workbook on the Rule of St. Benedict*. Trabuco Canyon, Calif.: Source Books, 1991.

de Vogüé, Adalbert, OSB. *The Rule of St. Benedict: A Doctrinal and Spiritual Commentary*. Translated by John Baptist Hasbrouck, OCSO. Kalamazoo: Cistercian Publications, 1983.

✓ de Waal, Esther. *Seeking God: the Way of St. Benedict*. Collegeville, Minn.: The Liturgical Press, 1984.

Ward, Benedicta, SLG. *The Wisdom of the Desert Fathers*. Fairacres, Oxford: SLG Press, 1986.

Wathen, Ambrose G., OSB. *Silence: The Meaning of Silence in the Rule of Saint Benedict*. Kalamazoo: Cistercian Studies, 1973.

White, James F. *Introduction to Christian Worship*. Nashville: Abingdon, 1981.

CISTERCIAN PUBLICATIONS, INC.

TITLES LISTINGS

CISTERCIAN TEXTS

THE WORKS OF BERNARD OF CLAIRVAUX

Apologia to Abbot William
Five Books on Consideration: Advice to a Pope
Grace and Free Choice
Homilies in Praise of the Blessed Virgin Mary
The Life and Death of Saint Malachy the Irishman
Love without Measure. Extracts from the Writings
    of St Bernard (Paul Dimier)
The Parables of Saint Bernard (Michael Casey)
Sermons for the Summer Season
Sermons on the Song of Songs I - IV
The Steps of Humility and Pride

THE WORKS OF WILLIAM OF SAINT THIERRY

The Enigma of Faith
Exposition on the Epistle to the Romans
Exposition on the Song of Songs
The Golden Epistle
The Nature of Dignity of Love

THE WORKS OF AELRED OF RIEVAULX

Dialogue on the Soul
The Mirror of Charity
Spiritual Friendship
Treatises I: On Jesus at the Age of Twelve, Rule for
    a Recluse, The Pastoral Prayer

THE WORKS OF JOHN OF FORD

Sermons on the Final Verses of the Songs of Songs I - VII

THE WORKS OF GILBERT OF HOYLAND

Sermons on the Songs of Songs I-III
Treatises, Sermons and Epistles

OTHER EARLY CISTERCIAN WRITERS

The Letters of Adam of Perseigne I
Baldwin of Ford: Spiritual Tractates I - II
Gertrud the Great of Helfta: Spiritual Exercises
Gertrud the Great of Helfta: The Herald of God's
    Loving-Kindness
Guerric of Igny: Liturgical Sermons I - II
Idung of Prüfening: Cistercians and Cluniacs: The
    Case of Cîteaux
Isaac of Stella: Sermons on the Christian Year
The Life of Beatrice of Nazareth
Serlo of Wilton & Serlo of Savigny
Stephen of Lexington: Letters from Ireland
Stephen of Sawley: Treatises

MONASTIC TEXTS

EASTERN CHRISTIAN TRADITION

Besa: The Life of Shenoute
Cyril of Scythopolis: Lives of the Monks of Palestine
Dorotheos of Gaza: Discourses
Evagrius Ponticus:Praktikos and Chapters on Prayer
The Harlots of the Desert (Benedicta Ward)
John Moschos: The Spiritual Meadow

Iosif Volotsky: Monastic Rule
The Lives of the Desert Fathers
The Lives of Simeon Stylites (Robert Doran)
The Luminous Eye (Sebastian Brock)
Mena of Nikiou: Isaac of Alexandra & St Macrobius
Pachomian Koinonia I - III
Paphnutius: A Histories of the Monks of Egypt
The Sayings of the Desert Fathers
Spiritual Direction in the Early Christian East (Irénée
    Hausherr)
The Syriac Fathers on Prayer and the Spiritual Life
    (Sebastian Brock)

WESTERN CHRISTIAN TRADITION

Anselm of Canterbury: Letters I - III
Bede: Commentary on the Seven Catholic Epistles
Bede: Commentary on the Acts of the Apostles
Bede: Gospel Homilies I - II
Bede: Homilies on the Gospels I - II
Cassian: Conferences I - III
Gregory the Great: Forty Gospel Homilies
Guigo II the Carthusian: Ladder of Monks and
    Twelve Mediations
Handmaids of the Lord: The Lives of Holy Women in
    Late Antiquity and the Early Middle Ages
Peter of Celle: Selected Works
The Letters of Armand-Jean de Rance I - II
The Rule of the Master

CHRISTIAN SPIRITUALITY

Abba: Guides to Wholeness & Holiness East & West
A Cloud of Witnesses: The Development of
    Christian Doctrine (D.N. Bell)
Athirst for God: Spiritual Desire in Bernard of
    Clairvaux's Sermons on the Song of Songs
    (M. Casey)
Cistercian Way (André Louf)
Drinking From the Hidden Fountain (Spidlék)
Fathers Talking (Aelred Squire)
Friendship and Community (B. McGuire)
From Cloister to Classroom
Herald of Unity: The Life of Maria Gabrielle
    Sagheddu (M. Driscoll)
Life of St Mary Magdalene and of Her Sister
    St Martha (D. Mycoff)
The Name of Jesus (Irénée Hausherr)
No Moment Too Small (Norvene Vest)
Penthos: The Doctrine of Compunction in the
    Christian East (Irénée Hausherr)
Rancé and the Trappist Legacy (A.J. Krailsheimer)
The Roots of the Modern Christian Tradition
Russian Mystics (S. Bolshakoff)
The Spirituality of the Christian East (Tomas Spidlék)
Spirituality of the Medieval West (André Vauchez)
Symeon The New Theologian: The Practical &
    Theological Chapters and the Three Theological
    Discourses
Tuning In To Grace (André Louf)

MONASTIC STUDIES

Community & Abbot in the Rule of St Benedict I - II
    (Adalbert De Vogüé)
Beatrice of Nazareth in Her Context (Roger
    De Ganck)
Consider Your Call: A Theology of the Monastic Life
    (Daniel Rees et al.)
The Finances of the Cistercian Order in the Fourteenth
    Century (Peter King)

TITLES LISTINGS

Fountains Abbey & Its Benefactors (Joan Wardrop)
The Hermit Monks of Grandmont
 (Carole A. Hutchison)
In the Unity of the Holy Spirit (Sighard Kleiner)
Monastic Practices (Charles Cummings)
The Occupation of Celtic Sites in Ireland by the Canons
 Regular of St Augustine and the Cistercians
 (Geraldine Carville)
The Rule of St Benedict: A Doctrinal and Spiritual
 Commentary (Adalbert de Vogüé)
The Rule of St Benedict (Br. Pinocchio)
Towards Unification with God (Beatrice of Nazar-
 eth in Her Context, II)
St Hugh of Lincoln (D.H. Farmer)
Serving God First (Sighard Kleiner)
Way of Silent Love
With Greater Liberty: A Short History of Christian
 Monasticism and Religious Orders

CISTERCIAN STUDIES

A Difficult Saint (B. McGuire)
A Second Look at Saint Bernard (J. Leclercq)
Bernard of Clairvaux and the Cistercian Spirit
 (J. Leclercq)
Bernard of Clairvaux: Man, Monk, Mystic
 (M. Casey) Tapes and readings
Bernard of Clairvaux: Studies Presented to Dom
 Jean Leclercq
Bernardus Magister
Christ the Way: The Christology of Guerric of Igny
 (John Morson)
Cistercian Sign Language
The Cistercian Spirit
The Cistercians in Denmark (Brian McGuire)
The Cistercians in Scandinavia (James France)
The Eleventh-century Background of Cîteaux
 (Bede K. Lackner)
The Golden Chain: Theological Anthropology of
 Isaac of Stella (Bernard McGinn)
Image and Likeness: The Augustinian Spirituality
 of William of St Thierry (D. N. Bell)
An Index of Cistercian Works and Authors in the
 Libraries of Great Britain I (D.N. Bell)
The Life of Ailred
The Mystical Theology of St Bernard (Etiénne
 Gilson)
Nicholas Cotheret's Annals of Citeaux (Louis J.
 Lekai)
The Spiritual Teachings of St Bernard of Clairvaux
 (J.R. Sommerfeldt)
Studiosorum Speculum
Wholly Animals: A Book of Beastly Tales (D.N.Bell)
William, Abbot of St Thierry
Women and St Bernard of Clairvaux (Jean Leclercq)

MEDIEVAL RELIGIOUS WOMEN

Lillian Thomas Shank and John A. Nichols, editors

Distant Echoes
Peace Weavers
Hidden Springs

STUDIES IN CISTERCIAN ART AND
ARCHITECTURE
Meredith Parsons Lillich, editor

Volumes I, II, III, IV now available

THOMAS MERTON

The Climate of Monastic Prayer (T. Merton)
The Legacy of Thomas Merton (P. Hart)
The Message of Thomas Merton (P. Hart)
Thomas Merton: The Monastic Journey
Thomas Merton Monk (P. Hart)
Thomas Merton Monk & Artist (Victor Kramer)
Thomas Merton on St Bernard
Thomas Merton the Monastic Journey
Toward an Integrated Humanity (M. Basil
 Pennington et al.)

CISTERCIAN LITURGICAL DOCUMENTS
SERIES
Chrysogonus Waddell, ocso, editor

The Cadouin Breviary (two volumes)
Hymn Collection of the Abbey of the Paraclete
Two Early *Libelli Missarum*
Molesme Summer-Season Breviary (4 volumes)
Institutiones nostrae: The Paraclete Statutes
Old French Ordinary and Breviary of the Abbey of
 the Paraclete: Text & Commentary (2 vol.)
The Twelfth-century Cistercian Psalter
The Twelfth-century Usages of the Cistercian Lay-
 brothers

STUDIA PATRISTICA
*Papers of the 1983 Oxford patristics conference
edited by Elizabeth A. Livingstone*

XVIII/1 Historica-Gnostica-Biblica
XVIII/2 Critica-Classica-Ascetica-Liturgica
XVIII/3 Second Century-Clement & Origen-
 Cappodician Fathers
XVIII/4 *available from Peeters, Leuven*

Cistercian Publications is a non-profit corporation. Its publishing program is restricted to
monastic texts in translation and books on the
monastic tradition.

*North American customers may order these books
through booksellers or directly from the warehouse:*
Cistercian Publications
St Joseph's Abbey
Spencer, Massachusetts 01562
(508) 885-7011
fax 508-885-4687

*Editorial queries and advance book information
should be directed to the Editorial Offices:*
Cistercian Publications
Institute of Cistercian Studies
Western Michigan University
Kalamazoo, Michigan 49008
(616) 387-8920
fax 616-387-8921

*A complete catalogue of texts in translation and
studies on early, medieval, and modern monasticism
is available at no cost from Cistercian Publications.*